BREAKTHROUGH TO WEALTH

SHARONTINE BOTTLEY

BREAKTHROUGH TO WEALTH

Berhune Publishing House Inc.

CONTENTS

DEDICATION

This book is lovingly dedicated to the four pillars of my foundation – my great-grandmother, Mary Eliza, whose quiet strength laid the groundwork for generations yet to come; my grandmother, Rocelia, who carried that strength with grace and purpose; my mother, Julia, who poured her wisdom into my becoming; and my daughter, Morgan Simone, the beautiful reason I reach higher and dream further.

You are my lineage, my legacy, and my greatest inspiration. To every woman standing at the intersection of capability and calling – you who feel the pull of something greater, yet sense that one vital piece remains just out of reach, this book was written for you. The missing component is not out there; it is within these pages, and more importantly, within you. Your breakthrough is not coming. It is here.

THE EXPENSIVE TRUTH
ABOUT PLAYING IT SAFE

Today is the beginning of my reality check as I sat in my car outside Chase Bank for forty-seven minutes, engine running, staring at the $127.83 in my checking account. Forty-seven minutes. I know because I watched every single one tick by on my dashboard clock, calculating how many days until payday, how many bills were already late, how many family members I'd have to dodge until I could make it right. Master's degree hanging in my home office. Six-figure salary on paper. And here I was, a grown woman with a corner office, afraid to go inside because I knew my debit card would decline on a $20 withdrawal. Finally realizing that my life was no longer serving me as I needed.

That's when the truth hit me like lightning on a clear day: Playing it safe had cost me everything.

Not all at once, mind you. Financial safety doesn't rob you dramatically. It pickpockets you slowly, one 'responsible' decision at a time. It whispers sweet lies about security while inflation eats your savings, while opportunities pass you by, while generational wealth builds in other families' accounts but never yours. It dresses up fear as wisdom and calls procrastination 'being careful.'

But here's what they don't tell you about playing it safe with money: It's the most dangerous game you can play.

Think about it. Our grandmothers saved every penny, stashed cash in coffee cans, I kept money 'just in case.' Beautiful intention, limited strategy. Because while that money sat there being 'safe,' it was actually losing value every single day. While we were being 'responsible' with our steady paychecks and savings accounts earning 0.01% interest, inflation was stealing 3-4% annually. Do the math, that's safe money? It's disappearing before your eyes.

You know what's really expensive? Watching your coworker, the one with half your qualifications, negotiate her third raise while you're grateful just to have a job. Expensive is discovering your colleague invested her bonus while you 'safely' paid off low-interest debt, and now her investment account has more zeros than your salary. Expensive is realizing you've been so busy avoiding financial risk that you've guaranteed financial regret.

I learned this the hard way, sitting in that parking lot, when I finally understood: My financial safety was actually financial sabotage wrapped in respectability.

The research backs this up with painful precision. A Stanford study of wealth accumulation patterns found that 'financially conservative' individuals, those who prioritize safety over growth, end up with 78% less wealth over a 30-year period than those who take calculated financial risks. Not 10% less. Not 20% less. Seventy-eight percent less. That's not a gap; that's a canyon.

But it gets worse. When researchers specifically studied Black women's wealth-building patterns, they discovered something heartbreaking: We're the most educated demographic in America, yet we hold less than 1% of the wealth. Why? Because we've been conditioned to survive, not thrive. We've been taught to be grateful for paychecks instead of building portfolios. We've been programmed to play it so safe that we're actually playing ourselves.

Here's the expensive truth nobody wants to say out loud: Every year you wait to invest is a year of compound interest you'll never get back. Every time you choose the 'safe' job over the entrepreneurial opportunity, you're choosing a ceiling over the sky. Every time you say 'I'll start building wealth when...' you're writing a check your future self can't cash.

The cost of playing it safe isn't just financial, it's generational. It's your children learning poverty mindsets instead of prosperity principles. It's your family tree growing the same fruit generation after generation because nobody was brave enough to plant different seeds.

I see you, sis. Sitting at your desk with your sensible salary and your sensible goals, wondering why sensible feels so much like stuck. You've done everything 'right'. You got the degree, climbed the ladder, contributed to your 401k, and kept your credit clean. Yet here you are, one unexpected expense away from financial chaos, one job loss away from starting over, one medical emergency away from a GoFundMe page.

That's not security. That's sophisticated struggling.

Real financial security doesn't come from avoiding risk; it comes from understanding which risks are worth taking. It doesn't come from one income stream you pray never dries up but it comes from multiple streams that flow regardless of who signs your paycheck. It doesn't come from playing small enough to avoid failure, it comes from playing big enough that failure becomes tuition, not tragedy.

The truly dangerous financial game? It's not the stock market. It's not real estate. It's not starting that business. The truly dangerous game is believing that trading your time for money for forty years while inflation eats your savings is somehow 'safe.' It's accepting that the path your mother walked really worked, save a little, struggle, repeat is the only path available to you. Not giving weight to the fact that in order to see change, there has to be a change.

Let me tell you what changed everything for me in that bank parking lot. I stopped asking, 'What if I lose?' and started asking, 'What if I never try?' I stopped calculating how much I could save by cutting coupons and started calculating how much wealth I was losing by not investing. I stopped being proud of my financial discipline and started being honest about my financial fear.

Because here's what financial safety really costs: It costs you the compound interest on investments you never made. It costs you the business profits from the company you never started. It costs you the real estate appreciation on properties you never purchased. It costs you the generational wealth that could have freed your children from ever sitting in a bank parking lot, afraid to check their balance.

The numbers are staggering when you really look at them. (Example)If you invest $500 monthly starting at 35 with a conservative 7% return, you'll have about $610,000 by 65. Wait until you're 45 to start 'playing it safe'? That number drops to $246,000. That ten-year delay − that decade of being 'careful' − cost you $364,000. That's not just money. That's freedom. That's a choice.

That's your children's college funds, your parents' care, and your ability to be generous without calculating.

But the cost goes beyond numbers. Playing it safe costs you confidence. Every time you choose security over growth, you're reinforcing the belief that you're not capable of more. You're teaching yourself that you're someone who needs protection, not someone who creates possibilities. You're practicing smallness instead of practicing wealth.

Here's what I discovered after I finally went into that bank: The riskiest thing I could do was keep doing what I'd been doing. The most dangerous choice was no choice at all. The most expensive decision was indecision. Because while I was being 'careful,' life was being expensive. While I was playing it safe, opportunities were passing me by. While I was avoiding failure, I was guaranteeing mediocrity.

That's the expensive truth about playing it safe: It's not safe at all. It's just familiar fear dressed up as wisdom.

You can feel that discomfort rising in your chest? That voice said, 'But what about...' That's not caution talking. That's conditioning. That's every message you've ever received about staying in your lane, being grateful for what you have, not getting 'too big for your britches.' That's generational programming that served our grandmothers in their time but is suffocating us in ours.

The world has changed, beloved. The rules have changed. What kept our ancestors safe is keeping us stuck. The job security our parents prayed for? It doesn't exist anymore. The pension plans they trusted? They're extinct. The social security they counted on? It's hanging by a thread. Playing by rules written for a world that no longer exists isn't safe; it's financial suicide in slow motion.

You know what's actually safe? Skills that pay regardless of who's signing checks. Income that flows whether you show up or not. Assets that are appreciated while you sleep. Knowledge that compounds faster than inflation.

Networks that open doors you didn't know existed. Investments that work harder than you ever could. That's not risky; instead, it should be viewed as revolutionary.

But revolution requires recognition. You have to see the prison before you can plan the escape. You have to admit that your financial comfort zone has become your financial cage. You have to acknowledge that every 'safe' choice is actually a dangerous delay of your wealth-building journey.

I'm not suggesting you gamble your rent money on cryptocurrency or quit your job without a plan. I'm not advocating for recklessness disguised as risk-taking. I'm talking about calculated risks – the kind that successful people take every day while we're busy being careful.

I'm talking about investing in your education and actually using it to build wealth. I'm talking about starting that side business while you still have your salary. I'm talking about buying assets instead of liabilities. I'm talking about betting on yourself like your life depends on it – because financially, it does.

The expensive truth about playing it safe is that it's a luxury we can't afford. Not in this economy. Not with these obligations. Not with these dreams. Not with ancestors who sacrificed everything so we could have opportunities they couldn't imagine. Playing it safe is playing small, and playing small is betraying every prayer ever prayed over your possibility.

So here's my challenge to you, right here in Chapter One: Calculate your real cost of playing it safe. Not just the obvious costs – the dreams deferred, the opportunities missed. Calculate the compound cost. The wealth that could have been built. The freedom that could have been yours. The legacy that could have been growing. Add it all up, every safe choice that led to a mediocre outcome, every careful decision that kept you exactly where you started.

Look at that number. Feel that weight. Let it make you angry. Let it make you ambitious. Let it make you active. Because that number? That's not your sentence – it's your fuel. That's not your failure – it's your tuition for the university of wealth building you're about to enter.

The expensive truth about playing it safe is that it has cost you enough already. The question isn't whether you can afford to take risks - it's whether you can afford not to.

Your breakthrough to wealth begins the moment you stop confusing busy with productive, safe with secure, and survival with success. It begins when you realize that the biggest risk you can take is not taking any risks at all. It begins when you decide that playing it safe has played you for the last time.

That day in the bank parking lot, I made a decision that changed everything: I would rather fail attempting wealth than succeed at staying poor. I would rather lose money learning to invest than lose decades being afraid to try. I would rather build imperfectly than plan perfectly and never begin.

Three years later, I had multiple income streams, investment accounts that grew while I slept, and enough savings that bank balances no longer triggered anxiety attacks. Not because I got lucky. Not because I had advantages you don't have. But because I finally understood that the expensive truth about playing it safe is that it's the most dangerous lie we tell ourselves about money.

Your ancestors didn't survive everything they survived for you to play it safe with their legacy. Your children aren't watching you to learn how to hide from opportunity. Your gifts weren't given to you to bury in the backyard of fear. Your breakthrough is waiting on the other side of your willingness to admit that safety isn't safe anymore.

The clock is ticking. Inflation isn't waiting for you to feel ready. Opportunity isn't pausing for your perfect moment. Wealth is being built by people with half your talent and twice your courage. The only question that matters is: How much more are you willing to pay for the illusion of safety?

Because now you know the expensive truth. Playing it safe has cost you everything you've been too afraid to reach for. But here's the beautiful flip side of that painful coin,– starting today, starting right now, starting with your next decision, you can stop paying that price. You can stop choosing familiar poverty over unfamiliar prosperity. You can stop letting fear dressed up as wisdom make your financial decisions.

Your breakthrough to wealth isn't waiting for the perfect moment, the perfect plan, or the perfect opportunity. It's waiting for you to realize that imperfect action beats perfect paralysis every single time. It's waiting for you to understand that the cost of playing it safe is a bill you can't afford to keep paying.

For Actionable results to avoid playing safe:

Your 5-Step Action Breakthrough

Step 1: Identify Your "Safe Zone" Write down one area where you've been playing it safe with your finances, career, or business.

Be brutally honest—what opportunity are you avoiding because it feels risky?

Step 2: Calculate the Real Cost List of what playing it safe in this area has already cost you (money, time, growth, opportunities). Project what it will cost you in 6 months, 1 year, and 5 years if nothing changes.

Step 3: Define One Imperfect Action. Choose one concrete action you can take within the next 72 hours. It doesn't need to be perfect—it just needs to move you forward. Make it specific and measurable.

Step 4: Set Your Commitment Write down your action, the exact date and time you'll do it, and share it with one person who will hold you accountable.

Step 5: Take the Action—Then Reflect Execute your imperfect action. Afterward, note what you learned. Imperfect action creates real data; perfect paralysis creates nothing.

Remember: Progress compounds. Your next breakthrough starts with this one imperfect step.

Welcome to your awakening. Welcome to your activation. Welcome to the first day of your wealth-building journey. The expensive truth about playing it safe is now your most valuable lesson. What do you do with that truth? That's Chapter Two of your story. And I promise you, it's going to be worth every risk you're finally ready to take.

WHEN YOUR DEGREE DOESN'T EQUAL YOUR WEALTH

The rejection email arrived at 11:47 AM on a Tuesday. After three rounds of interviews, a presentation that had executives nodding, and qualifications that exceeded every requirement, I didn't get the promotion. Again. The feedback was familiar – "You're doing great where you are." Translation: Stay in your place. The salary bump that would have finally let me breathe? Given to Mark, who had half my credentials but all the confidence of someone who'd never been told to be grateful just to be in the room.

I stared at my wall of degrees, including Bachelor's, Master's, and certifications that cost more than my car. Frames that my mother polished with pride every time she visited. Evidence of excellence that was supposed to be my golden ticket. Yet there I was, making less than contractors who learned their trade on YouTube. There I was, with more letters after my name than dollars in my savings.

That's when I finally understood: I'd been sold a lie wrapped in academic regalia.

Because here's what they don't tell you at graduation: Your degree opens doors, but it doesn't build wealth. It gets you in the room, but it doesn't get you the equity.

We were raised on the gospel of education. "Get your degree, and you'll be set." Our parents preached it, our teachers reinforced it, our communities celebrated it. And why wouldn't they? For them, education was the bridge from the fields to the office, from the factory to the boardroom. A degree was a revolution in their generation. In ours? It's barely evolved.

Don't misunderstand me, education transformed my life. It expanded my mind, challenged my assumptions, and gave me tools I use every day. But somewhere between the student loans and the salary negotiations, I discovered a brutal truth: Academic intelligence and financial intelligence are two completely different languages, and most of us are only fluent in one.

I watch my clients wrestle with this reality every day. Brilliant women with impressive resumes and unimpressive bank accounts. PhDs living paycheck to paycheck. MBAs are afraid to invest. Engineers who can solve complex equations but can't calculate their net worth. We mastered every subject except the one that determines whether we build wealth or just earn wages, money itself.

The statistics are sobering. The average college graduate earns $1.2 million more over their lifetime than someone with only a high school diploma. Sounds impressive until you realize that spread over 40 years, that's just $30,000 annually – before taxes, before student loan payments, before the real cost of "professional" living. Meanwhile, the average real estate investor builds more net worth in 5 years than most degree holders accumulate in 20.

But for Black women, the numbers tell an even starker story. We earn 61.1 bachelor's degrees for every 36.1 earned by Black men. We're the most educated demographic in America. Yet we hold less wealth than any other group.

How does the most educated become the least wealthy? Because education without a financial strategy is like having a powerful engine with no wheels – all that potential going nowhere fast.

The painful truth is that while we were studying for degrees, others were studying money. While we were memorizing theories, they were building assets. While we were earning grades, they were earning equity.

I'll never forget the day this hit home with crystal clarity. I was at a conference, sitting next to a woman who'd dropped out of community college. As I complained about the burden of student loans, she mentioned she'd just closed on her third rental property. When I asked how, she said simply, "I spent less time in classrooms and more time in rooms where deals get made."

That stung. Because I realized I'd been in educational rooms, corporate rooms, conference rooms, but rarely in wealth-building rooms. I knew how to write a thesis, but not a business plan that actually made money. I could analyze Shakespeare, but couldn't analyze an investment opportunity. I'd mastered academic success but remained financially illiterate.

The real betrayal isn't that education didn't deliver wealth; it's that it convinced us we didn't need to learn about money. After all, smart people with good jobs figure it out, right? Wrong. Intelligence without financial education is like having a map with no compass. You can see all the destinations, but have no idea how to reach them.

Here's what your degree actually bought you: access, credibility, and problem-solving skills. Valuable? Absolutely. Sufficient for building wealth? Not even close. Because wealth building requires a completely different curriculum, one that they don't teach in traditional classrooms.

You need to understand how compound interest works in your favor, not just in theory but in practice. You need to know why buying assets beats earning income every time. You need to recognize that your salary is just seed money for investments, not the harvest itself.

You need to master tax strategies that preserve wealth, not just earn it. These lessons? They're not in your textbook. They're in the accounts of people building wealth while you're building someone else's dreams.

The corporate game is rigged, beloved, and our degrees are just admission tickets to a game we're not equipped to win. They'll pay you enough to need the job but not enough to leave it. They'll promote you enough to feel progress but not enough to build power. They'll value your contribution at quarterly reviews but not in equity distribution.

This is the wealth gap that nobody talks about, not the gap between educated and uneducated, but the gap between those with degrees and those with financial intelligence.

I see it in my own journey. The year I finally started investing, I made more from my investment returns than from my annual raise. The rental property I was "too busy" to research while climbing the corporate ladder? It's appreciated more in three years than my salary has increased in ten.

The business I started on the side? It's now worth more than my entire retirement account from 20 years of corporate contributions.

But here's where it gets interesting. Your degree, properly leveraged, can be a wealth-building accelerator. The problem isn't the education, it's what we do with it after graduation. We use our degrees to get jobs instead of creating them. We use our knowledge to build other people's businesses instead of our own. We use our credibility to strengthen someone else's brand instead of building our legacy.

What if you used your nursing degree to start a home health agency? What if your teaching credential became the foundation for an education consulting firm? What if your MBA helped you acquire businesses instead of just managing them? What if your expertise became your equity?

The wealth-building education you need isn't another degree. It's understanding that income is not wealth; net worth is. It's knowing that good debt (that brings returns) beats being debt-free with no assets. It's recognizing that your time is not your most valuable asset; your knowledge properly monetized is. It's seeing that every dollar you earn has three jobs: live on some, invest some, and use some to create more.

Your degree taught you how to earn. Now you need to learn how to own. Your education showed you how to work. Now you need to learn how to build. Your credentials got you a seat at the table. Now you need to learn how to own the table.

The shift from employee mindset to owner mindset isn't comfortable. It requires admitting that everything you believed about career success might be incomplete. It means acknowledging that while you were being excellent at your job, others were being strategic about their wealth. It demands humility to learn what you don't know and courage to act on what you learn.

But here's the beautiful part – you already have what it takes. The discipline that earned your degree? Channel it toward financial education. The research skills from your thesis? Apply them to investment analysis. The presentation abilities you honed? Use them to pitch your business ideas. The network you built in school? Transform it into strategic partnerships. Your degree isn't worthless – it's just under-utilized.

The real return on your educational investment comes when you stop seeing your degree as the destination and start seeing it as transportation. When you stop letting your credentials define your ceiling and start using them to build your foundation. When you stop being proud of titles and start being strategic about ownership.

I think about that Tuesday afternoon, staring at that rejection email, and I'm grateful. Grateful it woke me up. Grateful it forced me to question why multiple degrees hadn't translated to multiple income streams. Grateful it pushed me to seek the education that actually builds wealth – the kind you get from mentors, not professors; from market experience, not academic theory; from trying and failing and adjusting, not from memorizing and repeating.

Today, my degrees still hang on my wall. But they're surrounded by property deeds, business licenses, and investment account statements. They remind me that formal education got me started, but financial education got me free. They represent not where I stopped learning, but where my real education began.

So here's my challenge to you: Stop letting your degree be your identity and start letting it be your tool. Stop using your education to qualify for jobs and start using it to create opportunities. Stop being the most educated and least wealthy and start being educated AND wealthy.

Your breakthrough isn't about devaluing your education – it's about adding to it. It's about saying, "I'm grateful for what this degree gave me, and I'm ready for more." It's about recognizing that you're not behind because you focused on education; you're positioned perfectly because now you can add financial intelligence to academic intelligence and create exponential results.

The truth when your degree doesn't equal your wealth? Your degree was never supposed to equal wealth. It was supposed to equal opportunity. What you do with that opportunity determines your wealth. Oh, and that next level of education, It starts the moment you close this chapter and open your mind to the lessons they never taught in school.

Because your ancestors didn't sacrifice for you to be an educated employee. They sacrificed for you to be educated AND empowered, degreed AND wealthy, credentialed AND creating generational impact. Your degree is just Chapter One of your success story. Your wealth-building journey? That's the rest of the book. And trust me, it's going to be a bestseller.

BREAKING THE STRONG BLACK WOMAN MONEY CURSE

We all can recount being on the other end of a call for help. It was 2 AM, voice trembling through tears she didn't want me to hear. My cousin Sylvia, the family rock, the one everyone turned to when life got lifey. "I can't do it anymore, Maya," she whispered. "Mama needs her medication, Tre's tuition is due, the car broke down, and I just... I can't. I've got seventeen dollars to my name and eleven days until payday. I'm so tired of being strong."

I knew that exhaustion in my bones. Not just physically tired but soul tired. Strong Black Woman tired. The kind that comes from carrying everyone's expectations on a salary that barely carries you. The kind that builds from saying yes to every family need while your own dreams suffocate in silence. The kind that accumulates when you're everyone's financial plan but nobody's financial priority.

That night, listening to Sylvia break, I recognized the sound of a curse breaking too. Not the supernatural kind our grandmothers warned about. The cultural kind we inherited without question – the Strong Black Woman Money Curse that says our strength is measured by how much we sacrifice, not how much we succeed.

Because here's what nobody tells you about being the Strong Black Woman: It's the highest-paying unpaid position in the world. You get all the responsibility with none of the equity. All the weight with none of the wealth.

We wear "strong" like a uniform we can't take off. Strong when the rent is due. Strong when family calls for help. Strong when our children need things we can barely afford. Strong when coworkers dump their work on our desks because we're "so good at handling things." Strong when everyone eats, while we fast. Strong when everyone rises, while we sink. Strong until strong becomes another word for drowning with a smile.

But let's pull back the curtain on this performance. The Strong Black Woman isn't just an identity; it's an economic system that depends on our free labor, our discounted dreams, and our subsidized sacrifice. It's a wealth extraction program disguised as a compliment. It's financial oppression dressed up as cultural pride.

Think about it. Who taught you that your worth was measured by how much you could endure, not how much you could enjoy? Who convinced you that taking care of yourself financially was selfish, but bankrolling everyone else was noble? Who decided that Black women's strength meant we didn't deserve soft landings, backup plans, or overflow accounts?

This conditioning starts early. We watch our mothers work multiple jobs, skip meals, and perform miracles with minimum wage.

We see them celebrated for "making it work" instead of being supported to make it better.

We learn that love looks like depletion, that family means financial martyrdom, that a good Black woman puts everyone else's oxygen mask on first, even when the plane is crashing.

By the time we're adults, the programming is complete. We automatically volunteer to cover the shortfall. We reflexively reach for our wallets when others reach out for help. We instinctively prioritize their emergencies over our investments. We've internalized that our financial purpose is to be everyone else's financial backup plan.

The curse shows up in ways we don't even recognize as problematic:

You keep your raise a secret because the family will expect more support. You hide your savings because visibility means vulnerability to requests. You downplay your success because shine attracts expectation. You postpone your dreams because someone else's crisis always seems more urgent. You accept less pay because you're "grateful to have a job." You give from your necessity instead of your abundance because that's what strong looks like, right?

Wrong! That's not strength, that's systematic wealth prevention. That's not love, that's enabling dressed in cultural drag. That's not honoring your ancestors; that's perpetuating patterns they prayed would end with you.

The research on Black women's giving patterns is staggering. We give away 12% of our income on average, compared to 3% for other demographics. But here's the kicker, we give from lower baseline incomes while carrying higher family obligations. We're literally giving ourselves broke while everyone around us builds wealth on the foundation of our sacrifice.

I learned this the expensive way when I realized I'd been an emergency fund for others but had no emergency fund for myself. I'd covered relatives' bills while my own sat in red. I'd been so strong for everyone else that I had no strength left to build my own wealth.

The breaking point came when I sat down, and something in me finally said

No to the pattern of continuously availing myself to others yet hurting myself in the process.

The Strong Woman Money Curse isn't about becoming heartless. It's about recognizing that you can't pour from an empty cup, and you damn sure can't build wealth from an empty account.

Here's the truth that will set your finances free: Being strong doesn't mean being stupid with money. Taking care of a family doesn't mean taking on their financial dysfunction. Loving your people doesn't mean financing their choices. Supporting others doesn't mean sacrificing your own stability.

Real strength – revolutionary strength – looks like building wealth so powerful that you can help from overflow instead of essence. It looks like creating systems that multiply what you have instead of dividing it among endless needs. It looks like modeling financial wisdom that models how to fish instead of just handing out fish sandwiches.

But breaking this curse requires more than mindset shifts. It requires practical strategies for protecting your wealth while still honoring your values:

The Boundary With Benefits: Set clear financial boundaries but attach them to benefits. "I'm not loaning money anymore, but I am willing to pay for financial literacy courses." This shifts the dynamic from enabler to empowerer.

The Time Release Technique: Never give money immediately. Institute a 48-hour consideration period. Amazing how many "emergencies" resolve themselves when you don't respond from emotional activation.

Breaking the Strong Black Woman Money Curse also means recognizing the voices that try to keep you bound:

"You think you're better than us now?" – No, you think you're better than broke.

"Family is supposed to help family." – Yes, help them learn to help themselves.

"It must be nice to have it like that." – It is nice, and it's available to anyone willing to change their patterns.

"You forgot where you came from." – No, you remember exactly where you came from, and you're determined not to stay there.

These voices aren't just external. The hardest ones to silence are internal, and the guilt that whispers you're being selfish, the fear that says you'll lose love if you stop giving, the shame that suggests wanting wealth makes you less spiritual, less connected, less Black.

But here's what I know for sure: You can't guilt your way to wealth. You can't shame your way to success. You can't sacrifice your way to abundance. The Strong Black Woman Money Curse thrives on these emotions, using them to keep you giving from lack instead of building toward overflow.

The antidote to this curse isn't weakness, it's wisdom. It's understanding that the strongest thing you can do is build wealth that outlasts any crisis. It's recognizing that modeling financial success does more for your family than enabling financial dependence.

It's knowing that every dollar you invest in your future is a dollar that compounds into generational change.

I think about my family member who made the 2 AM call now, two years after that 2 AM phone call. She took my advice and did the unthinkable – she put herself on her own payroll first. Automated her savings before the family could ask for it.

Started a side business instead of a second job. Said no to requests and yes to investments. Set boundaries that felt like betrayal but were actually breakthroughs.

Today? She still helps the family – from her overflow account designated for giving. She still supports others through the jobs her business creates. She still carries the family by showing them what's possible when you break the curse of sacrificial strength and embrace strategic wealth building.

The other day, she called me, voice steady and proud. "I just want you to know – I've got six months of expenses saved. My investment account hit five figures. And when Mama needed help last month, I wrote the check without checking my balance first. That's real strength."

She's right. Real strength isn't measured by how much you can endure but by how much you can build. Not by how empty you can become for others but by how full you can stay while lifting them up. Not by how well you can struggle but by how powerfully you can prosper.

Breaking the Strong Black Woman Money Curse isn't about becoming weak. It's about becoming wealthy. It's about transforming from everyone's financial sacrifice to your family's financial strategist. It's about evolving from the one who saves the day to the one who changes the game.

Your ancestors didn't survive everything they survived for you to be everyone's financial martyr. They survived for you to thrive. They sacrificed so you could succeed. They were strong so you could be strategic. They carried the weight so you could build wealth.

So here's your invitation to break the curse: Start saying no to financial requests that compromise your wealth building. Start saying yes to investments that multiply your ability to help. Start automating your wealth before others can access it. Start modeling what it looks like when a Strong Black Woman adds wisdom to her strength and builds something nobody can take away.

Because the strongest Black woman isn't the one who carries everyone, she's the one who builds systems that elevate everyone. She's not the one who gives until it hurts. She's the one who grows until it overflows. She's not the one who sacrifices her dreams for others' needs. She's the one who achieves her dreams and shows others how to achieve theirs.

The Strong Black Woman Money Curse ends with you. Not in weakness, but in wisdom. Not in selfishness, but in strategy. Not in disconnection from the community, but in building wealth that serves the community sustainably.

Break the curse. Build wealth. Become the ancestor who changed everything. Because strong is beautiful, but strategic is revolutionary. And wealthy? That's your birthright reclaimed.

Here's a tactical step guide to break free from that cycle:

Your 3-Step Liberation Guide

Step 1: Recognize the Pattern. Identify where you're carrying financial burdens alone that should be shared, delegated, or released entirely. Write down who or what you're financially supporting at the expense of your own wealth-building.

Step 2: Audit Your "Strength Level" Calculate what being "strong" is actually costing you—the extra jobs, the family support, the inability to ask for help, the opportunities you've sacrificed. Add up the real dollar amount over the past year.

Step 3: Create Your Boundaries. Identify one financial boundary you need to set this week. Practice this phrase: "I'm prioritizing my financial foundation so I can support from a position of strength, not depletion."

Your breakthrough: You can't pour from an empty cup. Building your wealth IS supporting your community.

THE GENERATIONAL WEALTH BLUEPRINT

Your Ancestors Prayed For This

The letter appeared in a dream so vivid I woke up tasting red dirt and hearing spirituals. My great-grandmother Mary Eliza stood at the edge of a cotton field, her hands bleeding from the bolls, writing with a stick in the dust: "Baby girl, I'm planting seeds I'll never see bloom. Working land I'll never own. Building wealth I'll never touch. But you... You're the harvest I'm praying for."

I sat up in bed at 3:17 AM, tears streaming, ancestors' presence thick as morning fog. The dream felt less like imagination and more like transmission – a direct download from the other side of struggle. I could see her face, weathered by sun and sorrow, lit by a hope so fierce it survived the Middle Passage, slavery, Jim Crow, and every attempt to extinguish it.

My great-grandmother, Mary Eliza, was one of the first black female entrepreneurs in her small town in Franklin Parish, Louisiana. She owned her own hair salon, and her brothers were barbers in the late 1800s. Her story is a testament to my entrepreneurial spirit that I inherited.

That's when I finally understood: My wealth-building wasn't just personal. It was a prophecy.

Because here's what hit me in that sacred hour between night and dawn: Every financial boundary I'd been afraid to set, every investment I'd been hesitant to make, every wealth-building opportunity I'd been too guilty to take — I wasn't just cheating myself. I was cheating on centuries of prayers.

We need to have a grown-up conversation about what our ancestors actually wanted for us. Not what we project onto their memory to justify our small living. Not what fear whispers to keep us comfortable in familiar struggle. But what they really dreamed in those moments when hope was all they had.

They didn't survive what they survived for us to romanticize poverty as culture. They didn't endure what they endured for us to wear financial struggle like a badge of authenticity. They didn't sacrifice what they sacrificed for us to feel guilty about wanting more than enough.

Let me paint you a picture with numbers that should make you weep and then make you wealthy: If your great-grandmother had been paid fairly for her domestic work — let's say just $15 per hour in today's dollars for 40 years of labor — she would have earned $1,248,000. If that money had been invested with just a 7% annual return, your family would have over $17 million today. Seventeen. Million. Dollars.

That's not fantasy. That's mathematics. That's what compound interest does when it has time and opportunity to work. That's what was stolen – not just wages, but wealth. Not just income, but an increase. Not just money, but multiplication across generations.

Your ancestors didn't lack work ethic. They lacked access. They didn't lack wisdom. They lacked opportunity. They didn't lack vision. They lacked rights. But you? You lack nothing but the decision to build what they dreamed.

I think about Mary Eliza in that cotton field, bending her back while envisioning my straight spine. Working land she couldn't own while dreaming of deeds with our family name. Building someone else's wealth while praying for our prosperity. She couldn't open a bank account, but she opened a spiritual trust fund that's been gathering interest in the realm of possibilities, waiting for someone to make the withdrawal.

That someone is you. That someone is me. That someone is every Black woman reading this who's been playing small while carrying ancestral-sized dreams.

The blueprint our ancestors prayed for wasn't complicated. They wanted simple things that seemed impossible then but are available now: To own instead of rent. To employ instead of beg for work. To invest instead of just surviving. To leave instead of just live. To multiply instead of just maintain. To choose instead of just cope.

But here's where we get it twisted: We think honoring them means struggling like them. We confuse remembering their pain with repeating their patterns. We mistake gratitude for their sacrifice with guilt about our success. We've turned their forced limitation into our chosen lifestyle.

Real ancestral honor looks like taking every opportunity they couldn't access. It looks like a building with every tool they couldn't touch. It looks like growing wealth with every strategy they couldn't study. It looks like becoming everything they dared to dream when dreaming was dangerous.

Sacred Economics isn't some new-age concept — it's an old-age truth. Our ancestors understood that money was energy, and energy was meant to flow, grow, and multiply.

They practiced sacred economics in sou-sou and saving circles, pooling resources to buy freedom, land, and futures. They understood that wealth wasn't individual, but it was communal. But they also understood that for wealth to lift communities, someone had to build it first.

You are that someone. You are the answered prayer. You are the freedom paper. You are the 40 acres. You are the mule. You are the reparations. No longer waiting to become them.

The sacred economics of ancestral wealth building has seven pillars, each one a direct response to what was denied:

First Pillar: Property Ownership. They were property; you become property owners. Every deed you sign rewrites the story of bodies sold on auction blocks. Your name on real estate transforms their names in the bill of sales. This isn't just an investment, it's a restoration.

Second Pillar: Business Equity. They built businesses with their hands and received no ownership. You build businesses that bear your name and build your wealth. Every LLC you form, every corporation you create, every trademark you file is a reclamation of creative power that was exploited without compensation.

Third Pillar: Investment Portfolios. They couldn't access banks, much less stock markets. You can buy pieces of every company in America with your phone. Every share you purchase is a share in the prosperity they were systematically excluded from. Your portfolio is their portion, finally paid.

Fourth Pillar: Intellectual Property. Their innovations were stolen, their creations appropriated. You can protect, monetize, and scale your ideas. Every patent, every copyright, every course you create transforms their uncompensated genius into your generational wealth.

Fifth Pillar: Education Funding. They risked death to learn to read. You can fund libraries of learning. Every 529 plan you open, every scholarship you fund, every book you write continues the lessons they started by candlelight.

Sixth Pillar: Estate Planning. They died with nothing to leave but love and lessons. You can create trusts that last for generations. Every will you write, every beneficiary you name, every legacy you legally protect, ensures your wealth outlives you like their prayers outlived them.

Seventh Pillar: Wealth Mindset. They had to think about survival; you get to think about sovereignty. Every abundance you think, every prosperity principle you practice, every wealth strategy you study upgrades the mental operating system from scarcity to plenty.

These aren't just financial goals – they're generational corrections. They're not just personal achievements – they're ancestral amendments. They're not just wealth-building strategies – they're prophecy fulfillment practices.

But let's be real about what building this blueprint requires. It means breaking the chains that feel like culture:

The chain of financial secrecy that our families whispered about money, as if it were shameful, instead of teaching it like it was sacred. Break it by talking openly about wealth, teaching transparently about building, and modeling abundantly about possibility.

The chain of crisis is always in emergency mode, never in empire mode. Break it by building buffers, creating cushions, and establishing systems that expect blessings, not just battles.

The chain of scarcity hoarding, holding so tight to little that there's no room for a lot. Break it by investing what you would have hidden, multiplying what you would have hoarded, and growing what you would have guarded.

Breaking these chains isn't betraying your bloodline, it's blessing it. It's not forgetting where you came from; it's finally going where they couldn't.

I need you to hear this in your spirit: Wanting wealth doesn't make you less Black. Building assets doesn't make you bourgeois. Creating generational prosperity doesn't disconnect you from the culture; instead, it demonstrates what the culture is capable of when finally given the chance.

Your ancestors' faith wasn't just about heaven later – it was about healing now. Their prayers weren't just for spiritual salvation; they were for physical liberation, economic elevation, and generational transformation. Every "Lord, make a way" was about money, too. Every "God, provide" included prosperity. Every "Jesus, help" hoped for wealth.

The blueprint they prayed for is in your hands. Not as a burden but as a blessing. Not as pressure but as privilege. Not as weight but as wings. You are the first generation with full access to:

Open any bank account

Start any business

Buy any stock

Own any property

Learn any skill

Build any dream

That's not a coincidence. That's coordination. That's not luck. That's legacy. That's not random. That's orchestrated. Your ancestors' prayers and your opportunities have finally found each other.

So here's what I need you to do – your Ancestral Wealth Declaration:

"I am Mary Eliza's dream made flesh. I am Rocelia's prayer made possible. Julia's hopes became real. I am the first of many. I am the breaker and the builder. I am the correction and the connection.

I will own land that my great-grandmother could only work. I will build businesses that my great-grandfather could only imagine. I will create wealth that my bloodline could only pray for. I will teach what they were forbidden to learn. I will document what they couldn't prove. I will protect what they couldn't keep.

My wealth is not about forgetting their struggle; it's about financing their dreams. My success is not about leaving them behind – it's about carrying them forward. My breakthrough is not about indi-

vidual achievement – it's about generational agreement with every prayer they prayed over the possibility.

I receive my role as the answer. I accept my assignment as the amendment. I embrace my position as the promise keeper. The blueprint is in my hands. The build begins today."

Write this declaration. Speak it daily. Live it boldly. Because faith without works is dead, but faith with wealth strategies? That's resurrection. That's restoration. That's reparations you pay yourself.

Your great-great-grandmother Mary Eliza? She's not just watching. She's working. Every investment you make, she's calculating compound interest in glory. Every property you purchase, she's preparing your mansion. Every business you build, she's opening doors in the spirit. Every generational pattern you break, every wealth principle you practice, every abundance move you make, heaven notices, ancestors rejoice, and the blueprint becomes building.

The generational wealth blueprint your ancestors prayed for isn't some distant dream you might achieve one day. It's an active assignment you're already qualified for. It's not about becoming worthy of wealth – you were born worthy. It's about becoming willing to build.

Because here's the secret they're whispering from glory: The wealth was never just about money. It was about options. It was about choices. It was about freedom. It was about the ability to say "YES" to a purpose without checking the price. It was about the power to build communities, fund dreams, and change narratives. It was about you becoming everything they dared to believe was possible when belief was all they had.

Your ancestors planted you in this moment. Your roots run deep through struggle, but your branches reach toward abundance. The blueprint is yours. The building begins now. The breakthrough to wealth isn't just personal achievement; it's prophecy fulfillment.

Build like they're watching. Because they are. Build like it matters. Because it does. Build like your great-great-granddaughter depends on it. Because she does.

The blueprint your ancestors prayed for is in your hands. What will you build with it? Their prayers have been answered. You're the answer. Now answer the call.

ASSETS OVER ACHIEVEMENTS-BUILDING WHAT MULTIPLIES

As the year comes to an end, I observed that the quarterly review numbers were perfect. Customer satisfaction: 98%. Team performance: exceeded every metric. My evaluation: "exceptional contributor." My raise: 2.7%.

I sat across from my regional director, watching him explain how lucky I was to get "above average" while inflation ate 3.5% of my purchasing power. That's when one of my colleagues, Marcus, texted me: "Closed on the duplex. Rent from unit 2 covers the whole mortgage. Building wealth while I sleep now."

BTW, this colleague and I share the same start date, same department, and significantly less "exceptional" according to our reviews. But while I was collecting accolades, he was acquiring assets. While I was perfecting performance metrics, he was purchasing properties. While I was climbing ladders, he was constructing foundations.

The drive home that day felt like a funeral procession for my illusions. Twenty-two years of being told "good job," fifteen years of exceeding expectations, a wall full of "Employee of the Month" plaques, and what did I have to show for it? A salary that felt like a leash and achievements that paid in compliments instead of compound interest.

That's the moment I finally understood: I'd spent my whole career building an impressive resume when I should have been building recurring revenue. I'd mastered the art of achieving when I needed to learn the science of acquiring.

The trap is so perfectly designed, you don't even realize you're in it. From kindergarten, they train us to chase gold stars, good grades, and glowing reviews. We learn that achievement equals worth, that recognition equals success, and that climbing equals progress. Nobody mentions that the ladder might be leaning against the wrong wall.

For high-achieving Black women, this trap has extra locks. We're not just chasing achievements, we're proving we belong. Every degree, every promotion, every award feels like evidence that we've made it. But made it to where? To higher taxes and longer hours? To fancier titles that don't translate to financial freedom? To corner offices in buildings we'll never own?

Here's the mathematical brutality of achievement versus assets: My annual 3% raise on a $75,000 salary equals $2,250 more per year. Marcus's duplex appreciating at 5% annually on a $200,000 property equals $10,000 in equity – plus $1,200 monthly in rental income.

My raise: taxed immediately, spent gradually, gone completely. His assets: appreciating constantly, cash-flowing monthly, building wealth generationally. I am grateful that my colleague's moves were a clear-cut example of what planning and managing your assets looks like. I later messaged him, extending my gratitude just for sharing.

The fundamental difference? Achievements make you valuable to others. Assets make you valuable to yourself. Achievements get you paid. Assets get you wealthy. Achievements require your presence. Assets work in your absence.

But understanding this intellectually and rewiring your entire operating system are two different battles. We're addicted to achievement because it gives us immediate validation. That promotion announcement, that LinkedIn congratulations flood, that salary increase – they trigger all the dopamine responses we've been trained to crave.

Assets? They're quiet builders. Nobody applauds when you buy your first share of stock. There's no ceremony for opening a business LLC. Your mortgage payment doesn't come with performance reviews. Assets build wealth in silence while achievements make noise.

The shift from achievement to asset mindset requires understanding four fundamental truths:

Truth #1: Your Salary Has a Ceiling, Assets Have Sky No matter how exceptional you are, there's a limit to what any job will pay you. But assets? A business can scale infinitely. Real estate can appreciate indefinitely. Investments can compound exponentially. Your exceptional performance might get you 10% raises. Exceptional assets can deliver 1000% returns.

Truth #2: Time Trading Always Has Limits. You have 24 hours. Subtract sleep, commute, and basic life maintenance – you may have 12 hours to monetize. That's your ceiling when you trade time for money. Assets break this equation. They work all 24 hours. They earn while you sleep, vacation, and live. They multiply time instead of consuming it.

Truth #3: Achievements Depreciated, Assets Appreciate. That Employee of the Year award from 2018? Nobody cares. That promotion from five years ago? Old news. That degree from a decade past? Table stakes now. Achievements lose value over time. But that rental property from 2018? Worth 40% more. That stock portfolio from five years ago? Doubled. That business from a decade past? Generational wealth now.

Truth #4: You Can't Inherit a Job, You Can Inherit Assets. Your children can't receive your VP title in your will. Your grandchildren can't deposit your performance reviews. Your legacy can't be built on what you achieved for someone else's company. But assets? They transfer. They compound. They create opportunities for people you'll never meet. They build legacies that last longer than lifetimes.

The psychology of shifting from achievement to assets is like learning to breathe underwater. Everything in you screams it's unnatural, until you realize you were always meant to swim in deeper waters.

I remember my first asset acquisition paralysis. Sitting with $10,000 saved, knowing I should invest, but terrified to move. What if I lost it? What if I chose wrong? What if everyone was right and "people like us" shouldn't play these games? My achievement brain wanted guarantees, certificates of success, and immediate validation. Asset building offers none of that, only–just the promise of eventual exponential returns.

The breakthrough came when I realized I was already an expert at taking risks – I just called them "career moves." I'd relocated for promotions, taken pay cuts for "better opportunities," invested thousands in degrees with no guaranteed return. The only difference? Those risks built other people's wealth. These risks would build mine.

Here's your Asset Acquisition Starter Pack:

The Business Builder Path: You don't need a revolutionary idea. You need a problem you can solve repeatedly for profit. That expertise you're giving away at your job? Package it. That skill everyone always asks you about? Monetize it. Start with one client, one product, one service. Build systems that deliver without your constant presence. Scale what works, eliminate what doesn't.

The Property Pioneer Path: You don't need hundreds of thousands. You need a strategy. House hacking – live in one unit, rent the others. FHA loans – as little as 3.5% down. Partner with other investors. Start with a small multi-family. Let tenants pay your mortgage while you build equity. Real estate has created more millionaires than any other asset class for a reason.

The Portfolio Pioneer Path: You don't need to understand every stock. You need to understand compound interest. Start with index funds – instant diversification. Automate monthly investments. Ignore daily fluctuations. Think decades, not days. $500 monthly invested at 8% annual return becomes $745,000 over 30 years. Not exciting daily, revolutionary eventually.

The compound effect changes everything. One of my colleagues started with one digital course teaching project management. Year one: $10,000 revenue. Year two: refined the course, $35,000. Year three: added coaching, $75,000. Year four: licensed the content, $150,000. Year five: built a full education company, $400,000. Same expertise she used at her job, but now it's an asset for building wealth instead of just earning wages.

Here's what nobody tells you about the moment assets start working: It feels like magic. That first month when rental income exceeds expenses. That first quarter when investment returns surpass your raise. That first year, when business revenue doubles without doubling your hours. You realize you've broken the time-for-money equation that keeps most people trapped forever.

But let's be honest about what this transition requires. You'll need to:

Embrace delayed gratification in a world of immediate consumption. Your coworkers will vacation while you invest. They'll upgrade cars while you acquire assets. They'll laugh about your "side hustles" until those hustles become your main income.

Accept imperfect action over perfect planning. Analysis paralysis is the response of the brain trying to protect you from asset risk. Your first property won't be perfect. Your first business will be messy. Your first investments will feel scary. Start anyway.

Prioritize ownership over optics. That title bump might impress at reunions, but that rental property builds wealth. That corner office might feel successful, but that business equity creates freedom. That promotion announcement might get likes, but that investment portfolio gets you retirement.

Transform from consumer to creator. Every purchase becomes a question: Could I own this instead of buying it? Could I create this instead of consuming it? Could I invest in this company instead of just shopping there? You start seeing ownership opportunities everywhere.

The shift accelerates when you realize assets compound more than financially – they compound psychologically. Owning assets changes how you see yourself. You're no longer just an employee hoping for raises. You're an investor expecting returns. You're not just climbing ladders. You're building empires. You're not just achieving. You're acquiring.

My 90-day foundation looked like this:

Week 1-2: Calculated my true net worth (assets minus liabilities) and cried. Listed every achievement that hadn't created assets and got angry. I researched one asset opportunity and got excited.

Week 3-4: Opened a separate investment account. Reduced dining out by 50% to fund it. Joined a real estate investment group to learn.

Week 5-6: Took an online course on stock investing. Created a business plan for monetizing my HR expertise. Toured three rental properties to understand the market.

Week 7-8: Made first $500 investment in index funds. Registered LLC for consulting business. Submitted offer on duplex (rejected but educated).

Week 9-12: Landed first consulting client. Investment account up 3%. Submitted second property offer with better terms.

Not perfect. Not massive. But moving. From achievement to assets, from employee to owner, from building a resume to building wealth.

Here's what I know now that I wish I knew then: Your

achievements got you to the room, but your assets let you buy the building. Your degrees opened doors, but your investments build houses. Your titles impress people, but your equity impresses banks.

The cruel irony? Once you start building assets, achievements come easier. When you don't need the job desperately, you negotiate better. When you have other income, you take bigger career risks. When you own things, you understand business differently. Assets don't replace achievements – they make them matter more because they're choices, not necessities.

Today, my wall still displays those certificates and awards. But they're surrounded by business licenses, property deeds, and investment statements. The achievements remind me how hard I can work. The assets remind me how smart I can be.

Your breakthrough moment isn't when you get your next promotion. It's when you realize that promotion is just seed money for your next asset. It's when you stop seeing your salary as success and start seeing it as startup capital. It's when you transform from someone who achieves for others into someone who acquires for yourself and your lineage.

Because here's the final truth: Achievements tell the story of where you've been. Assets write the story of where you're going.

Achievements make you proud of your past. Assets make you powerful in your future. Achievements die with you. Assets live beyond you.

So make the shift. Start the acquisition. Build the portfolio. Create the empire. Not because achievements don't matter, as we all know that they do, but because achievements plus assets are equally unstoppable. Unstoppable is exactly what your breakthrough to wealth requires.

The question isn't whether you can achieve it. You've already proven that. The question is whether you'll acquire it. Whether you'll build. Whether you'll shift from being exceptional at building other people's dreams to being strategic about building your own wealth.

Your future self – the one with assets generating income, properties building equity, and investments compounding continuously – is waiting for you to stop achieving your way to exhaustion and start acquiring your way to abundance.

The shift from achievements to assets isn't just a financial strategy. It's a freedom strategy. It's a generational strategy. It's a "never have to choose between purpose and payment" strategy.

Choose assets. Choose multiplication. Choose wealth that works without you. Choose freedom that funds itself. Choose a legacy that lasts forever.

Because achievements might make you memorable, but assets make you unforgettable. And unforgettable wealth? That's what breakthroughs are built on.

CREATE MULTIPLE STREAMS NOT MULTIPLE BREAKDOWNS

When we think of achieving more, it goes hand in hand with doing more. Multiple streams of income are equivalent to multiple streams of insanity.

I'd bought into the hustle hard mythology. Every guru preached it: "You need seven streams of income!" "Diversify or die!" "Sleep is for people who don't want wealth!" So there I was, wanting wealth so badly I hadn't slept properly in months.

Running five side hustles that collectively earned less than one focused business could have. Building multiple streams that were really just multiple leaks draining my energy, time, and sanity.

I wasn't building multiple streams of income. I was building multiple streams of exhaustion that happened to occasionally produce money.

That's when it hit me: There's a difference between multiple streams and multiple demons. Between diversification and desperation. Between building wealth and building burnout.

Are the gurus selling the "hustle harder" narrative? They weren't teaching wealth building. They were teaching wealth hemorrhaging disguised as productivity.

Here's what nobody tells you about the multiple streams gospel: Most millionaires didn't get there by doing seventeen things poorly.

They got there by doing one or two things exceptionally well, then letting those successes fund additional streams that could run without consuming their souls.

But for Black women especially, the pressure to create multiple streams comes from a real place – we know how quickly single income sources can disappear. We've watched our mothers get laid off after decades of loyalty.

We've seen our communities devastated by plant closures and industry shifts. Multiple streams feel like protection against a world that's proven it won't protect us.

The key isn't avoiding multiple streams; it's building them strategically instead of desperately. It's understanding that true income streams should multiply your money, not your misery. It's recognizing that sustainable wealth building requires systems, not just sweat.

Real multiple streams are like rivers flowing into your lake of wealth. Fake multiple streams are like holes poked in your bucket, draining faster than you can fill.

Enter the STREAMS framework, it's the new filter for evaluating whether an income opportunity is a wealth builder or a time thief:

Scalable: Can this grow without proportionally growing your time investment? A freelance gig where you trade hours for dollars? Not scalable. A course you create once and sell repeatedly? Scalable. If it can't grow beyond your personal bandwidth, it's a job, not a stream.

Time-leveraged: Does this generate income beyond the hours you actively work? Driving for Uber only pays while you're driving. Rental property pays while you're sleeping. If income stops the moment you stop, it's a hustle, not a stream.

Renewable: Does this provide ongoing returns or one-time payments? A freelance project ends when it is delivered. A membership site renews monthly. If you're constantly hunting for the next sale, you're surviving, not thriving.

Expert-aligned: Does this leverage knowledge you already possess? Starting a candle business when you're a financial analyst? That's creating new work. Selling financial planning templates? That's leveraging existing expertise. Use what you know, don't learn from zero.

Asset-based: Are you building something you can eventually sell or that builds equity? Your Uber car depreciates. Your online business appreciates it. If it's not building value beyond immediate income, it's consumption, not investment.

Manageable: Can this fit within your life without destroying it? If adding this stream means never seeing your family, never resting, never enjoying life, then the money won't matter. Wealth without wellbeing is just well-paid misery.

Synergistic: Do your streams strengthen each other? If your consulting clients become course customers who buy your book and join your membership, that's synergy. If each stream requires completely different audiences, skills, and systems – that's insanity.

Score each opportunity against all seven criteria. Less than 5 out of 7? It's probably a time trap, not a wealth stream. This framework saved me from countless "opportunities" that would have drained my energy for minimal return.

The magic happens when you limit yourself to three complementary streams instead of juggling seven competing ones.

Here's the three-stream sweet spot that actually builds wealth:

Stream 1 – Your Stability Stream: This is your enhanced primary income. Maybe it's your job where you've negotiated remote work to save commute time and costs. Maybe it's your main business that covers your core expenses. This stream provides the foundation that lets you build others without desperation.

Stream 2 – Your Growth Stream: This is your scalable asset with expansion potential. The rental property that appreciates while generating income. The online business that can grow beyond your direct involvement. The investment portfolio builds compound returns. This stream has no ceiling.

Stream 3 – Your Passive Stream: This requires minimal ongoing maintenance. Dividend-paying stocks. Licensing your intellectual property. High-yield savings for your emergency fund. This stream works while you focus on the others.

Notice what's missing? The seventeen different hustles that have you running in circles. The random opportunities that sound good but don't fit your expertise. The time-intensive gigs that keep you too busy to build real wealth.

My colleague Rashida models this perfectly.

Stream 1: Her cybersecurity job pays $105,000.

Stream 2: Her cybersecurity consulting firm serving small businesses, now generating $180,000 annually.

Stream 3: Investing her profits in index funds and REITs, producing $20,000 in annual passive income. Three streams. One expertise. Zero burnout. Total income: $305,000.

Compare that to her friend Nicole: Full-time job, Uber on weekends, MLM products, freelance graphic design, weekend catering, online tutoring, and flipping items on Facebook Marketplace. Seven streams. Seven different skill sets. Constant exhaustion. Total income: $75,000.

The difference? Rashida built streams. Nicole built stress. Rashida created systems. Nicole created chaos. Rashida has wealth and well-being. Nicole has multiple jobs and mounting frustration.

But here's what changes everything: Systems and automation.

The wealthy don't work harder – they build better systems. Every stream should eventually run with minimal input from you. This requires upfront investment in:

Financial Systems: Separate bank accounts for each stream. Automated transfers to savings and investments. Accounting software tracks everything. Quarterly reviews instead of daily panic. You can't manage what you don't measure, and you can't scale what you can't systematize.

Time Systems: Batch similar tasks. Content creation on Mondays. Client calls on Tuesdays. Financial reviews on Fridays. When you context-switch constantly, you lose 25% of your productivity to mental transitions. Themed days create focused flow.

Communication Systems: Email templates for common inquiries. FAQ pages prevent repetitive questions. Virtual assistants handling routine communications. Calendly eliminates back-and-forth scheduling. Your time is too valuable for administrative exhaustion.

Growth Systems: Documented processes anyone can follow. Training materials for delegation. Standard operating procedures for quality control. If it requires your constant presence, it's not a system; it's a job with yourself as the boss.

The investment in systems pays exponentially. My virtual assistant costs $400/month but saves me 20 hours. My automated email sequences took a week to write, but generate sales daily. My property management company takes 8% but eliminates landlord headaches. Systems are the difference between multiple streams and multiple jobs.

Energy management becomes crucial. Different streams require different energy: Creative energy (content creation, product development)

Analytical energy (investment research, financial planning)

Relationship energy (client management, networking)

Physical energy (property maintenance, product fulfillment)

Map your streams against your energy patterns. I create content in the morning when I'm mentally fresh. Client calls happen in the afternoon when I'm social but not creative. Investment

research happens on Sunday mornings with coffee and quiet. Fighting your natural energy rhythms guarantees burnout.

Real talk: The first year of building proper streams is hard. You're investing time and money in systems while managing current obligations. You're saying no to quick money to build long-term wealth. You're watching others vacation while you build. But by year two? Those systems start working. By year three? You're making money while you vacation.

The integration effect is when your streams stop competing and start completing each other.

My transformation timeline:

Month 1: Evaluated all current "streams" against the STREAMS criteria. Alleviated four time-wasters.

Month 2: Systematized remaining work. Hired the first VA. Automated what I could.

Month 3: Launched consulting using existing expertise. Three clients from the network.

Month 6: Consulting income exceeded side hustle chaos. Alleviated two more time-wasters.

Month 9: Invested consulting profits in real estate partnerships. True passive income.

Month 12: Three solid streams generating 2x my previous seven-hustle income.

The difference was profound. Instead of being everywhere poorly, I was strategic excellently. Instead of responding to every opportunity, I filtered through the framework. Instead of multiple breakdowns, I had multiple breakthroughs.

Your 6-month stream launch plan starts with one question: What expertise do you already have that others need? Not what's trendy. Not what's easy. What do you know that solves expensive problems?

Month 1: Choose your Stream 2 based on expertise. Research the market. Validate demand.

Month 2: Build basic systems. Legal structure. Financial separation. Simple automation.

Month 3: Pilot launch. Three to five beta customers. Gather feedback. Refine offering.

Month 4: Official launch. Focused on systems, not scale. Document everything.

Month 5: Optimize based on data. Delegate repeatable tasks. Increase prices.

Month 6: Evaluate and decide: Scale, maintain, or pivot. Begin exploring Stream 3.

Notice what's missing? The frantic hustle. The sleepless nights. The sacrifice of everything that matters for money that doesn't last. Building wealth through multiple streams isn't about doing more – it's about building better.

Because here's the truth: Multiple streams without systems is just multiple jobs. Multiple streams without a strategy are just a sophisticated struggle. Multiple streams without sanity is just wealthy misery.

The goal isn't to be busy, it's to be building. Not to have multiple jobs, but to have money multiplied. Not to hustle harder but to hustle smarter. Not to sacrifice your life for streams but to have streams that fund your life.

I think about that Thursday night, missing dinner with Denise for the fifth time, drowning in hustle culture's lies. Now? My streams run whether I work or rest. They grow whether I'm grinding or grateful. They pay whether I'm present or on vacation.

That's the difference between multiple streams and multiple breakdowns: One builds wealth while building a life. The other builds income while destroying everything else.

Choose streams over stress. Choose systems over hustle. Choose strategic over scattered. Choose three excellent over seven exhausting. Choose wealth that includes well-being.

Your breakthrough to multiple streams isn't about doing more. It's about building better. It's about income that flows without drowning you. It's about wealth that works harder than you do. It's about freedom that funds itself.

Stop building multiple breakdowns. Start building multiple breakthroughs, because the only thing better than money that flows is a life that flows with it.

INVESTMENT INTELLECT
FOR THE CULTURE

While most are ultra conservative when it comes to investing, we tend to avoid the risk of investing at all. Well, on this bright Monday morning, my co-worker flashed an envelope that was thin, generic, the kind that usually holds bills or bad news.

But when my coworker opened it that Tuesday morning, her scream shattered the windows. "EIGHT HUNDRED THOUSAND DOLLARS!" She held up her 401 (k) statement, hands shaking, tears streaming.

We gasped, gathered around, stared at those numbers like they were foreign languages. She's usually very soft-spoken, however on this day, we all heard the loud gasp. She worked in accounting and earned the same salary range as us, same struggles, same complaints about making ends meet.

"How?" That's all I could manage.

"I started investing when I was 25," she said quietly. "Just $200 a month in index funds. Every month for 30 years. I never touched it. Never even looked at it much. And now..." She trailed off, staring at her future in black and white.

That's when the room split in two. Half of us leaned in, hungry for details. The other half leaned back, arms crossed, suspicious. "It must be nice to have that kind of money to invest." "The market is rigged anyway." "That's basically gambling." "Not for people like us."

I watched my colleague's face change. From joy to something sadder, heavier. Like she'd broken some unspoken rule by winning a game we'd all agreed not to play.

That night, I couldn't sleep. Eight hundred thousand. From $200 a month. While I'd been "safely" saving in my 0.01% interest savings account, my colleague had been quietly building wealth that could change her entire lineage. While I'd been repeating stories about the market being "for them, not us," she had been proving those stories wrong.

The investment gap between us and wealth isn't made of missing money – it's made of missing education, missing representation, and missing the compound interest on every year we wait to begin.

Let me hit you with numbers that should make you angry enough to act: The average white American family has 68% of their wealth in investments. The average Black family? 33%. That gap isn't about intelligence or capability. It's about access to information, historical exclusion, and inherited fears that masquerade as wisdom.

Every time we say "I don't trust the stock market," we're right to be cautious. Our grandparents were systematically excluded from wealth-building opportunities. Our parents watched Black Wall Street burn. We've seen our communities redlined out of real estate appreciation and priced out of business ownership. The mistrust is earned.

But here's what staying out costs us: If you invest $300 monthly starting at 30 with a 7% annual return, you'll have about $789,000 by 65. Start at 40? That drops to $304,000. That decade of "I don't trust it" just cost you $485,000. Nearly half a million dollars. That's not caution — that's catastrophe.

The market doesn't care about your trust. Compound interest doesn't wait for your comfort. Wealth builds for those who participate, regardless of their feelings about the invitation.

But let's demystify this whole thing. Strip away the suits and the jargon and the deliberate complexity designed to keep us out. At its core, investing is simply owning pieces of things that make money. That's it. Not gambling. Not guessing. Owning.

When you buy stock in Apple, you own a tiny piece of every iPhone sold. When you invest in a real estate fund, you own a piece of buildings collecting rent. When you buy bonds, you're basically being the bank, loaning money and collecting interest. It's ownership, simplified and accessible.

Think about it like this: You know that feeling when your favorite restaurant is packed and you think, "They must be making money"? Investing lets you own part of that money-making. You know how your apartment building collects rent from every unit? Real estate investment trusts (REITs) let you be on the collecting side. You know how banks make money lending? Bonds let you play bank.

But for us, investing can't just be about returns. It has to align with our values, support our communities, and build wealth without selling our souls. Enter the Cultural Wealth Code – investing that multiplies money and meaning.

Values-Based Investing Options That Actually Pay:

ESG Funds (Environmental, Social, Governance): These invest in companies doing good while doing well. Clean energy. Diversity in leadership. Community development. Returns? Often matching or beating traditional funds. Your money grows while supporting what you believe in.

Community Development Financial Institutions (CDFIs): These are banks and credit unions specifically focused on serving underserved communities. You can invest in CDs earning 3-5% while your money funds Black businesses, affordable housing, and community development. It's like keeping your money in the community while still earning returns.

Black-Owned Business Investments: From publicly traded companies like Carver Bancorp to private investments in Black-owned businesses through platforms like Republic, you can directly support while building wealth. The beauty? These often outperform because they're serving markets traditional investors ignore.

Impact Real Estate: REITs focused on affordable housing, senior living, or community development. You earn quarterly dividends while your investment improves communities instead of gentrifying them.

The myth that you have to choose between values and returns is exactly that – a myth. Sustainable investing has matched or outperformed traditional investing consistently. Turns out, companies that treat people and the planet well tend to perform well. Shocking, right?

But knowing about options and actually investing are two different battles. So let's build your personal investment blueprint based on where you are right now:

The Cautious Builder Path (for the "I don't trust it" crew):

Start here if the market feels scary and you need baby steps. Your blueprint:

Target-date funds: Set it and forget it. The fund automatically adjusts as you age. Broad index funds: Own tiny pieces of every major company. When the market grows, you grow. Start with $50-100/month. Automate it so you don't overthink it.

Expected returns: 6-8% annually over time

Peace of mind: Maximum. You're diversified across thousands of companies.

The Balanced Growth Seeker Path (for the "I'm ready to learn" squad):

You want growth but with guardrails. Your blueprint:

60% in index funds (stability)

20% in REITs (real estate exposure without landlord hassles)

10% in value stocks (companies you believe in)

10% in bonds or high-yield savings (safety net)

Expected returns: 7-10% annually

Learning curve: Moderate. You'll research but not obsess.

The Strategic Wealth Multiplier Path (for the "Let's build an empire" warriors): You're ready to accelerate wealth building. Your blueprint:

40% growth stocks and sector funds

30% real estate syndications or REITs

20% index funds for stability

10% alternative investments (peer-to-peer lending, cryptocurrency)

Expected returns: 10-15% annually (with more volatility)

Engagement level: High. You're actively learning and adjusting.

The path you choose matters less than choosing a path. My colleague Patricia didn't have a perfect strategy. She just had a consistent one. Time in the market beats timing the market every time.

But I know you're still sitting there with all the "but what ifs." So let's knock down every barrier between you and building investment wealth:

"But I don't have enough money to start." You can open an investment account with $1. Literally. One dollar. Apps like Acorns round up your purchases and invest the change. Fidelity and Schwab have zero minimum accounts. The "not enough money" excuse is dead. Bury it.

"But I don't understand it." You didn't understand driving until you learned. You didn't understand your job until you trained. Everything is incomprehensible until you begin. Start with one index fund. Learn about that one thing. Understanding grows with exposure, not avoidance.

"But what if I lose everything?" Diversified investing over time has never resulted in total loss. Ever. The market has crashed, but it has always recovered higher. Always. Your savings account? That's guaranteed to lose to inflation. That's the loss you should fear.

"But my family says it's gambling." Show them Patricia's statement. Gambling is hoping to beat odds stacked against you. Investing is owning businesses that produce value. Gambling is entertainment. Investing is building. They're opposites, not synonyms.

"But what if there's another crash?" There will be. Multiple crashes over your investing lifetime. And? Crashes are sales. When the market drops 30%, you're buying quality companies at discount prices. Crashes are how patient investors build wealth faster.

Let me walk you through your first investment week, hour by hour:

Day 1 (2 hours): Education baseline. Watch "Index Funds Explained" on YouTube. Read one article about compound interest. Feel your mind start to shift.

Day 2 (1 hour): Pick your platform. Vanguard, Fidelity, or Schwab for beginners. User-friendly, low fees, excellent education. Open an account online.

Day 3 (30 minutes): Fund your account. Transfer what you can. Even $25. Motion creates momentum.

Day 4 (2 hours): Research one investment. I recommend starting with a total market index fund. Reads like "VTSAX" or "FZROX." Own pieces of every public company in America with one purchase.

Day 5 (30 minutes): Make your first purchase. Buy your chosen fund. Feel the shift from consumer to owner. Screenshot it. This is your wealth-building birthday.

Day 6 (30 minutes): Set up automation. Monthly transfers and investments. Remove emotion and decision fatigue. Wealth builds on autopilot.

Day 7 (1 hour): Create a tracking system and celebrate. You're an investor now. No matter how small you started, you started. That's everything.

The compound effect visualization that changes everything:

$200/month from age 30 to 65 = $379,000

$200/month from age 25 to 65 = $622,000

Those five years of "I'll start later"? It costs you $243,000.

$500/month from age 30 to 65 = $948,000

$500/month from age 25 to 65 = $1,555,000

Those five years? It costs you $607,000.

This isn't about shame for not starting earlier. It's about urgency for starting now. Every month you wait is compound interest you'll never recover. Every year you avoid investing thousands, possibly millions, and you're choosing not to have.

But here's what makes my entire soul light up: When Black women invest, we don't just build wealth, we model possibility. We normalize ownership. We break generational patterns of exclusion. We fund our businesses, our communities, our dreams. We become the representation that the next generation doesn't have to search for.

One of my friends casually weighed in during one of our conversations that she started investing casually three years ago. $300 monthly into index funds and REITs. Nothing fancy. Nothing flashy. Last month, her 16-year-old daughter asked, "Mom, can you teach me about the stock market? I want to start investing my babysitting money."

THAT is how generational wealth begins. Not with millions. With mindset shifts. With mothers modeling. With compound interest working while we sleep.

Your investment intelligence isn't about becoming Warren Buffett. It's about becoming Consistent. Patient. Participating. Building wealth so gradually that it seems sudden.

Your Investment Success System moving forward:

Monthly (30 minutes): Review your investments. Not to panic sell, but to see growth. Watch compound interest work. Adjust contributions if you can increase.

Quarterly (1 hour): Rebalance if needed. Learn one new investment concept. Read one investment book. Your education compounds like your money.

Annually (2 hours): Review your strategy. Celebrate your growth. Increase contributions with raises. Set next year's goals. You're building an empire, thinking.

Continuously (1 hour/week): Education never stops. Podcasts during commutes. YouTube videos while cooking. Investment books instead of Netflix sometimes. Knowledge pays the best interest.

Find your investment community. Online groups, local investment clubs, friends building wealth. Isolation kills more investment dreams than market crashes. Community creates accountability and courage.

Create your Investment Emergency Kit:

Market crash plan: Remember, crashes are sales. Don't sell. Maybe buy more.

Job loss plan: Six-month emergency fund before aggressive investing.

Family pressure plan: Scripts for explaining why you're investing instead of being available. Doubt attack plan: Reread Patricia's story. Review your growth. Remember your why.

Here's my declaration for you to make yours:

"I am an investor. Not someday, but today. Not when I have more – with what I have. I own pieces of companies benefiting from my brilliance, my labor, and my consumption. My money multiplies while I rest because I decree it. I build wealth the same way wealthy people do – through ownership, patience, and compound interest. The market doesn't care about my fears, so I invest despite them. My ancestors couldn't access these tools. I can. That's not privilege – that's responsibility, I accept with gratitude and strategy. My investing journey begins now."

The expensive truth about avoiding investment? It's the most expensive decision you'll ever make. More expensive than any student loans. More costly than any credit card debt. More devastating than any financial mistake. Because mistakes can be recovered from. Time cannot be.

But here's the beautiful flip side: Starting today, even with $50, even with fear, even with imperfect knowledge, you join the ownership class. You begin building wealth that works all 24 hours.

You create freedom that funds itself. You model what's possible when Black women stop watching wealth build and start building it ourselves.

Patricia showed me something on Tuesday that changed every-thing: The market isn't for them. It's for anyone brave enough to enter. Wealth isn't for them. It's for anyone patient enough to build. Compound interest isn't for them. It's for anyone wise enough to start.

The gap between you and investment wealth isn't made of miss-ing millions. It's made of one missing decision: to begin.

Make it. Today. Now. Your future millionaire self is waiting for you to stop overthinking and start owning. Because investment intel-ligence for the culture isn't about perfection — it's about partici-pation.

And your participation? It changes everything.

THE BOUNDARY BANKING REVOLUTION

Wisdom had set in by now, and the realization that in order to see a change, we have to be the change. The text came at 6:47 AM on a Saturday. "Hey sis, my light bill is $287. Can you help? Kids need lights for homework" My cousin's third request this month.

Right after I'd transferred money for her "emergency" car repair and "one-time" help with groceries. I stared at my phone, thumb hovering over the Cash App, while my own daughter asked if we were going to her Saturday science program – the one I'd been saying we couldn't afford.

That's when the pattern finally became clear as lightning against a dark sky. There had been three generations of women in my family who had all been playing the same role: The Responsible One. The One Who Made It. The Family ATM.

I could see it stretching back – my mother funding her siblings while we ate struggle meals, my grandmother sending money home while wearing shoes held together with duct tape. And here I was, continuing the legacy, teaching my daughter that everyone else's emergency mattered more than our dreams.

As I began to reflect on the generational patterns, the tears came hard and honestly. Poverty is real, and utilities matter. But because I finally saw the trap: In trying to be the Strong Black Woman who saves everyone, I was ensuring none of us would ever be saved. I was perpetuating the very cycle I thought I was breaking.

The three-generation trap isn't just about money moving from your account to theirs. It's about dreams deferred becoming dreams denied, temporary helping becoming permanent dependency, and crisis management becoming culture.

I did the math that morning, and it broke me. Over the past five years, my retirement account sat at $31,000. While my daughter's college fund held $5,000. While my emergency fund stayed empty because every emergency was someone else's.

But here's what haunted me most: Fast-forward fifteen years. My daughter, who's now in medical school, I wanted to break the generational cycle that had existed way too long in this family. Stop the cycle from spinning forward, done in the power of love.

That Saturday morning, while doing some old-fashioned soul searching, I made a decision that was actually a breakthrough moment: I realized then that implementing new spending policies was a necessity. I needed to implement building systems that could actually sustain help instead of just sustaining struggle.

Enter the Boundary Banking Revolution – a complete reimagining of how we handle financial support. Not from a place of selfishness, but from strategic love. Not cutting people and systems off, but cutting off patterns that keep everyone stuck.

The Boundary Banking System has four accounts, each with its own rules, its own purpose, and its own protection:

The Foundation Account (70% of your income): This is YOUR wealth building. Untouchable. Non-negotiable. This funds your investments, your retirement, your property purchases, and your business building. This is the oxygen mask you put on first. Anyone who calls you selfish for protecting this doesn't understand that poverty isn't love – it's just a shared limitation.

The Family Fund (15% of your income): This is what you CAN give without guilt or depletion. When it's gone for the month, it's gone. Period. This isn't cruelty, – it's mathematics. It's the difference between helping for decades versus depleting in years. $500/month you can sustain beats $2000 you can't.

The Opportunity Account (10% of your income): This transforms handouts into hand-ups. Money here comes with requirements: business plans for ventures, enrollment proof for education, and accountability for outcomes. You're not just giving money – you're investing in transformation. The cousin who wants to start a business gets seed funding and mentorship, not just cash.

The Emergency Reserve (5% of your income): TRUE emergencies only. Death, health crises, and homelessness prevention. One-time per situation. Must have documentation. No repeating "emergencies" that are really just poor planning renamed. This preserves your ability to help when help really matters.

Setting this up changed everything, but not without battle. The first month, I had to say: "I love you AND my family fund is depleted for this month. I can help again next month if the need remains." The pushback came swift and sharp.

"It must be nice to have it like that." "You switched up now that you got a little something." "Family is supposed to help family." "You forgot where you came from."

Each accusation is designed to trigger guilt. Each one was a test of whether my boundaries were real or just theory. But I'd prepared. I'd written my responses, practiced them, believed them:

"I haven't forgotten where I came from. I remember so clearly that I'm determined to go somewhere else. And I want to take you with me – but as partners, not dependents."

Here's the thing about setting financial boundaries with family: You're not just changing your behavior. You're challenging an entire system that depends on extraction. You're disrupting patterns that feel like culture but are really just dysfunction dressed in tradition.

The scripts saved me. When emotion runs high, preparation runs the show:

For the initial boundary setting: "I love you, and I'm restructuring how I handle money to ensure I can help my family long-term instead of short-term. Let me explain the new system..."

For the guilt trips: "Being strategic with money means I can help for decades instead of being depleted in years. This is actually the most loving thing I can do."

For the "must be nice" energy: "It IS nice to build something sustainable. Let me show you how to do the same..."

For the emergency requests: "I understand this feels urgent. I have specific criteria for my emergency fund. Let's see if this qualifies and explore other solutions if not..."

The business investment asks: "I'm excited about supporting family businesses! Send me your business plan and let's schedule a time to discuss properly."

But boundaries without internal work are just performances. The guilt doesn't disappear because you memorize scripts. It transforms only when you understand that boundaries aren't walls — they're architecture for sustainable support.

The Guilt-Release Protocol became my daily practice:

Every morning, I listed what guilt was costing — not just money, but wealth multiplication. That $72,000 invested over five years could have been $100,000. That could have funded ten family members' business starts instead of ten thousand temporary fixes.

I calculated the true cost of being the family savior: Stress-induced health issues. Sleepless nights. Resentment building. Dreams deferred. Relationships strained by financial tension. My daughter learned that women sacrifice while everyone else lives.

I visualized the alternative future: Family members empowered, not enabled. Businesses built, not bills paid. Education funded, not emergencies covered. Generational wealth, not generational dependency.

The guilt didn't disappear, but it transformed from driver to passenger. Still present but no longer steering.

Six months in, something beautiful happened. Instead of just boundaries, I started building bridges – new ways of supporting that created dignity and development:

The Family Investment Club: Every family member could contribute whatever they could – even $25/month. We'd pool money and invest together. First month: eight members, $400 total. By year-end: fifteen members, $1500/month being invested. People who'd never thought about investing were now checking their portfolios, learning together, building together.

Financial Education Gatherings: Monthly Zoom calls where I taught what I was learning. Credit repair. Investment basics. Business building. Turns out people wanted knowledge more than handouts. My aunt, who always needed "gas money," started her meal prep business after our entrepreneurship session.

Business Incubator Approach: Instead of giving cousin Jerome $500 for "bills," I paid for his LLC formation and first month of business services for his lawn care idea. Requirement: weekly check-ins and financial reporting. That $500 turned into a business now employing three people.

The Scholarship Fund: Instead of random education help, created a formal family scholarship with applications, requirements, and celebrations. Kids had to maintain grades, volunteer, and write essays about their goals. Made education support feel like achievement, not charity.

Property Partnerships: Instead of giving rental assistance repeatedly, partnered with my brother to buy a duplex. He manages it, I funded down payment, we split profits. Now he's building equity instead of begging for help.

The resistance to these new models was fascinating. Some family members were angry about "requirements" and "paperwork." As if dignity was too high a price for help. But others? Others came alive. They'd been waiting for an invitation to build, not just survive. They'd wanted partnership, not pity.

My cousin, the one from the morning text that started it all, initially called me "bougie" and "funny acting." But three months later, she approached me quietly: "Can you teach me that investment stuff? I'm tired of always asking. I want to have something."

That's when I knew: Boundaries aren't rejection. They're the highest form of love. They say, "I believe you're capable of more than a crisis. I believe we can build wealth, not just share struggle. I believe in us enough to change the pattern."

The compound effect of boundaries shocked me. Year one was hard, lots of conflict, lots of guilt, lots of adjustment. Year two, things shifted. Family members started solving problems differently, knowing the bank was closed but the investment office was open. Year three, transformation:

Four family businesses launched with Opportunity Account funding

Family Investment Club portfolio worth $27,000

Six young people in college with Scholarship Fund support

Two rental properties owned in partnership with family

Fifteen family members are actively investing

More money helped families in three years of boundaries than five years of free-flowing giving. But more importantly, mindsets shifted. Conversations changed from "Can you help me pay..." to

"What do you think about this business idea..." Independence increased. Dignity multiplied. The family's financial culture transformed.

Not everyone made the journey. Some family members stay committed to crisis, addicted to emergency, invested in staying stuck. They faded from my life, replaced by family members ready to build. That's okay. Boundaries reveal who wants transformation versus who wants transactions.

My daughter watches all this, absorbing new patterns. She sees me help the family from strength, not depletion. She watches boundaries create better relationships, not broken ones. She's learning that loving your family doesn't mean financing their dysfunction. She's witnessing what happens when one woman decides the generational pattern stops with her.

The 30-day implementation plan for your own Boundary Banking Revolution:

Week 1: Internal foundation. Calculate your giving history. Feel the weight of it. Envision the alternative. Practice boundary statements in the mirror. Prepare for pushback.

Week 2: System creation. Open separate accounts for each fund. Set percentages. Create automatic transfers. Draft your Family Fund rules. Design your Opportunity Account requirements.

Week 3: Strategic communication. Tell your partner/children first – get aligned at home. Then one trusted family member who might support you. Then broader family, using prepared scripts. Expect resistance. Stand firm.

Week 4: Implementation and adjustment. First requests under the new system will test you. Use your scripts. Document decisions. Celebrate boundary wins. Adjust based on reality, not guilt.

Daily practices that sustain boundaries:

Morning affirmation: "My boundaries are bridges to better."

Evening review: "Did I honor my boundaries today?"

Weekly system check: Are the accounts balanced correctly?

Monthly evaluation: What's working? What needs adjustment?

Here's your Boundary Declaration:

"I commit to building wealth while loving my family. My boundaries aren't walls against connection – they're architecture for sustainable support. I release guilt about strategic giving. I embrace my role as a cycle breaker, pattern interrupter, and generational game changer. I will help from overflow, not essence. I will teach independence, not dependence. I will model what's possible when love includes limits and support includes structure. The old patterns end with me. The new patterns begin today. I am the boundary that becomes the bridge to everything we've been praying for."

Your breakthrough isn't choosing between family and wealth. It's understanding that without boundaries, you'll have neither. With boundaries, you can have both – family relationships that thrive and wealth that makes thriving possible.

The Boundary Banking Revolution isn't about becoming heartless. It's about becoming strategic. It's about loving your family enough to stop enabling patterns that keep everyone poor. It's about building wealth that serves sustainably instead of giving a guaranteed limitation.

The strongest position to help from is standing on solid ground, not sinking in quicksand. The most loving thing you can do is model what's possible when someone breaks the pattern. The most generous gift you can give is showing them how to fish, while the old system just passes out fish sandwiches until they run out.

Set the boundaries. Build the systems. Transform the patterns. Become the ancestor who changed everything – not by giving more, but by building better.

Your family needs your boundaries more than they need your money. Because your boundaries teach them what your money never could: how to build their own.

The Three-Generation Trap

As I stared at my reflection in the bathroom mirror at my cousin's baby shower, my hands were trembling slightly as I processed what had just happened. At 45, I had watched three generations of women in my family play out the exact same financial drama, and for the first time, I saw the pattern with devastating clarity.

The First Scene: Age 25

Twenty years earlier, at my grandmother's 70th birthday party, I had watched my mother quietly slip $200 to Uncle Jerome for his car repair. Then another $150 to cousin Tasha for her light bill. Before the evening ended, my mother, Julia, had handed out over $500 to various family members—money which I knew came from my mother's already stretched teacher's salary.

"Mama, why do you always give money to everybody?" I had whispered during the car ride home.

My mother, Julia's response was swift and certain: "Baby, family takes care of family. When you have more, you give more. That's just how we do it."

I remembered feeling proud of my mother's generosity, even as I noticed our own grocery budget getting tighter that month. It seemed noble, sacrificial, the right thing to do.

The Second Scene: Age 35

Fast forward to my daughter Jasmine's 10th birthday party. I, now a successful marketing manager making $85,000 a year, found myself in my mother's exact position. Uncle's son needed to borrow money—$1,500. Cousin's daughter needed help with rent—$800. My brother Marcus needed a loan for his latest business venture—$3,000.

By the end of that month, I had given away $5,300. I told myself it was temporary, that I was in a better position to help than my mother had been. But when I went to add money to Jasmine's college fund, the account sat at a disappointing $2,847. For a child who would be college-bound in eight years.

"I'm doing better than Mama did," I rationalized. "I make more money, so I can help more." But something nagged at me when I looked at that college fund balance.

The Third Scene: Age 45 - The Pattern Revealed

And now, twenty years after watching my mother, I stood at that baby shower watching my 25-year-old daughter Jasmine—fresh out of graduate school with her first real job at $65,000 a year—hand $400 to the same cousin (now asking for her granddaughter's school clothes) and promise another $200 to our Uncle's grandson for his car insurance.

The recognition hit me like a physical blow. I wasn't looking at three separate incidents. I was looking at the same scene, played out across three generations, with the only difference being the dollar amounts and the faces getting older.

My mind started calculating, and the numbers made my stomach turn over just how much I had gifted, not loaned, over the past ten years. I had given away approximately $180,000 to family members. Not loans—gifts. Money that never came back, money that if invested in an index fund averaging 7% returns, would now be worth over $350,000.

Three hundred and fifty thousand dollars. Jasmine's entire college education. A down payment on a rental property. The beginning of generational wealth. Gone.

But the real gut punch came when I realized the pattern: each generation was earning more than the last, but none of them were building more wealth. My grandmother cleaned houses and raised five children on that income. My mother cleaned houses and became a private nurse while she raised four children, always broke despite a steady paycheck. I made six figures and had only one child, yet I was still living paycheck to paycheck, just with better stuff.

The Inheritance We Don't Talk About

As I stared at my reflection in the bathroom mirror at my cousin's baby shower, my hands were trembling as I finally understood what my family had been passing down for generations.

It wasn't jewelry. It wasn't property. It wasn't money.

It was something far more powerful and far more destructive: an invisible inheritance of beliefs that made wealth impossible.

The Hidden Will

At 45, I had just watched my 25-year-old daughter Jasmine hand $400 to cousin Tasha with the same automatic response, the same apologetic smile, the same inability to say no that had defined three generations of women in my family.

At that moment, I realized that my family had a will—an unwritten, unspoken set of rules passed down from grandmother to mother to daughter like an heirloom no one wanted, but everyone kept.

And Jasmine had just inherited it.

Article I: You Are the Safety Net

Twenty years earlier, at my grandmother's 70th birthday party, even though I was young, I had absorbed the first clause of this invisible will: Your worth is measured by what you give, not what you keep.

I watched my mother, Julia, distribute $500 to family members that evening. But what I really inherited wasn't the act of giving—it was the belief that made it mandatory.

My mother had learned it from her mother, who cleaned houses and never said no to family in need. My grandmother would say, "Baby, we all we got," and what she meant was: Your money isn't really yours. It belongs to the family. You're just the current custodian.

This inheritance came with an unspoken commandment: If you have it and they need it, you give it. No questions. No limits. No exceptions.

I didn't choose this belief. I inherited it. It lived in my bones before I had language for it.

The Revelation

Sitting in my car after the party, I called my financial advisor. "Janet, I need you to run a scenario for me. What if I had invested $18,000 a year for the past ten years instead of giving it to the family?"

The number Janet gave me was brutal and beautiful at the same time: $265,000 in investments, not counting compound growth. Add in the compound interest, and I was looking at over $350,000 in wealth that could have been.

But more devastating was Janet's next calculation: "Maya, if you continue this pattern, you'll reach retirement with about $127,000 in your 401k and maybe $50,000 in other assets. Your monthly Social Security will be about $2,100. You'll be dependent on family support in your old age, just like—"

"Just like my grandmother was," I finished, the cycle suddenly crystal clear.

I sat in my car for another hour, crying for the first time in years. Not tears of sadness, but tears of recognition and, surprisingly, relief. I finally saw what I couldn't see before: I wasn't breaking generational cycles of poverty; I was perpetuating them with a bigger checkbook.

The families that had generational wealth—the ones I admired from afar—didn't just make more money. They protected their money. They had boundaries. They said no. They invested in assets, not just assistance.

The Decision

That night, I made a declaration to myself, standing in my mirror with the same determination my ancestors had shown when they decided to leave the South, when they decided to integrate schools, when they decided their children would have better lives:

"The buck stops with me. Literally. I will not pass this pattern to Jasmine. I will not reach old age because I was generous. I will not continue to confuse enabling with love."

I understood now that the most loving thing I could do for my family was to break the cycle. Not by cutting them off, but by changing the rules of engagement. By showing them what it looked like when a Black woman built wealth while still being family-oriented.

I was about to become something my family had never seen: a boundary-setting, wealth-building, legacy-creating Black woman who refused to choose between loving my family and securing my future.

The revolution was about to begin.

FAITH, FINANCE, AND FINDING YOUR CALLING

The Scripture hit differently at 2 AM. I'd been crafting my business plan, calculator in one hand, Bible in the other, trying to reconcile what felt like competing truths. "For the love of money is the root of all evil," stared back at me from 1 Timothy, while my bank statement showed $423, and my daughter needed school supplies tomorrow. Next to it lay my vision board, covered with affirmations about abundance, property deeds I'd claim, and businesses I'd build.

Was I losing my soul trying to gain wealth? Was building financial freedom somehow betraying my faith? The enemy had me in a theological headlock, using holy words to keep me broke, sanctifying my struggle while the prosperity promised throughout Scripture seemed reserved for everyone but me.

That's when the Holy Spirit whispered what religion had been too frightened to say: "Baby, your poverty isn't piety. It's poor stewardship of my provision."

I sat straight up, feeling the weight of revelation. All these years, I'd been confusing lack with holiness, struggle with spirituality, and financial stress with faithful living. But what kind of witness bounced checks? What testimony came from teaching my daughter that following God meant forever struggling? How was I glorifying Him by burying the talents He gave me under religious excuses?

The truth that set my finances free: God didn't design you for poverty. He designed poverty to be defeated by people like you who carry His power and wisdom. Your wealth isn't worldly — it's worship when aligned with His will.

That night launched my journey to understand the true marriage of faith and finance. I went back to Scripture with fresh eyes, seeking truth beyond tradition. What I found revolutionized everything:

"Beloved, I wish above all things that thou mayest prosper and be in health, even as thy soul prospereth" (3 John 1:2). Above ALL things. Not as a side note. Not as a maybe. As a primary desire of God for His children. "The blessing of the LORD, it maketh rich, and he addeth no sorrow with it" (Proverbs 10:22). Rich. Not just spiritually, but Rich and Joyfully so.

"But remember the LORD thy God: for it is he that giveth the power to get wealth" (Deuteronomy 8:18). Power to get wealth. Not guilty about wanting it. Power to build it.

Suddenly, I saw what tradition had hidden. The Bible is full of wealthy believers who used their resources for Kingdom impact. Abraham was a real estate mogul. Job was a livestock billionaire. David had treasures beyond counting. Lydia sold purple cloth to the elite. The Proverbs 31 woman ran multiple businesses while caring for family.

They weren't wealthy despite their faith. They were wealthy because their faith included financial wisdom. They understood that money is simply a tool, and like any tool, its virtue depends on the hands that wield it.

But here's what changed everything: understanding the Calling-Cash Connection. Your calling – that divine purpose burning in your spirit – requires capital to fully manifest. Moses needed resources to lead the exodus. Nehemiah needed funding to rebuild the walls. Even Jesus had a treasurer because ministry requires money.

What Kingdom assignment are you carrying that needs funding? What community problems could you solve with resources? What generational cycles could you break with wealth? What ministries could you launch, what schools could you build, what families could you transform if money weren't your limitation?

I think about Dr. Renee, the pediatrician, who called to address healthcare disparities in Black communities. Her calling required more than compassion – it needed capital. She built wealth through her practice and real estate investments, then opened free clinics in underserved areas. Her money became her ministry tool.

Or Marcus, the educator whose calling was reforming how Black children learn. Teaching alone couldn't fulfill it. He needed resources to create schools, develop curriculum, and train teachers. His business success funded his calling. Twenty schools later, thousands of children are thriving because he understood that calling without capital is just a nice idea.

Your calling isn't separate from your cash – they're divinely designed to work together. The wealth you build isn't a deviation from purpose – it's fuel for purpose. Every investment property can house someone needing shelter. Every business can employ someone needing opportunity. Every dividend can fund someone's breakthrough.

Stop letting religious tradition teach you that God is honored by your limitation. He's honored by your multiplication. The parable of talents wasn't about being grateful for little – it was about growing what you're given.

The spiritual practices that integrate faith with finance transformed my journey:

Morning Money Prayers: "Lord, I thank You for the resources You've entrusted to me. Give me wisdom to multiply them for Kingdom impact. Show me investments that align with Your will. Lead me to opportunities that serve Your purposes while building wealth."

Investment Intercession: Before every investment decision, I pray. Not just for profit, but for purpose. "God, if this investment honors You and serves Your people, let it prosper. If not, close the door clearly." He's answered both ways, saving me from losses and leading me to gains.

Business Blessings: Every venture gets dedicated to a divine purpose. My real estate investments house families while building wealth. My course sales fund scholarships. Business becomes ministry when oriented correctly.

Abundance Affirmations: Scripture-based declarations that rewire poverty programming. "I am the head and not the tail. I lend and do not borrow. Wealth and riches are in my house. I have more than enough to be a blessing. My God supplies all my needs according to His riches in glory."

The breakthrough came when I understood generous wealth building. The Overflow Principle changed everything: The more wealth you build, the more you can give. And here's the divine paradox, – the more you give from multiplication, the more multiplication accelerates.

Consider the math of generous building:

Same percentage. Exponentially different impact. Which glorifies God more – struggling to tithe hundreds or joyfully giving hundreds of thousands?

Strategic giving multiplies impact:

Donating appreciated stock avoids capital gains tax while funding the ministry

Creating donor-advised funds builds giving assets that serve perpetually

Business tithing from gross revenue demonstrates faith while reducing taxable income. Legacy planning ensures wealth serves God's purposes beyond your lifetime

Sister Michelle models this beautifully. Started with nothing but faith and vision. Built a consulting firm serving nonprofits. As revenue grew, so did her giving. Now she:

Funds an entire youth program at her church

Provides business grants to formerly incarcerated women

Sponsors twenty children's education in Ghana

Created an endowment for pastoral care

Her wealth is her worship. Her success is her service. Her prosperity is her platform for purpose.

Finding your financial ministry means discovering where divine calling meets monetary multiplication:

Ask yourself:

What injustices make my spirit burn?

What problems do I see that money could solve?

What communities could I serve with resources?

What Kingdom work needs funding that I could provide?

What would I do if money were no obstacle?

That last question reveals calling. Because calling exists beyond current capacity. It requires faith for the funding and funding for the fulfillment.

My financial ministry emerged from my pain point – watching brilliant Black women struggle financially despite their gifts. Now I teach wealth building as worship, helping sisters understand that their prosperity is part of God's plan. Every woman who breaks generational poverty patterns through my teaching multiplies Kingdom impact.

Your financial ministry might be:

1. The accountant teaching financial literacy as discipleship
2. The realtor helping families build generational wealth through homeownership
3. The investor funding Kingdom entrepreneurs

4.   The business owner employing the formerly incarcerated The wealth builder teaching prosperity with purpose

Making peace between your faith and finances requires rejecting false choices: You don't choose between prayer and profit – you pray for a profitable purpose. You don't choose between worship and wealth – you worship through wealth well-used. You don't choose between spiritual and successful – you succeed spiritually and financially. You don't choose between holy and wealthy – you build holy wealth that honors Him.

Daily declarations throughout:

"My wealth serves worship. My success serves souls. My prosperity serves a purpose. I build with blessing. I multiply with meaning. I prosper with peace."

Here's your Financial Faith Statement:

"I declare that my faith and finances are divinely aligned. I reject the religious lie that poverty proves piety. I embrace God's desire for me to prosper in all things. My wealth building is worship when wedded to His will. My success is service when submitted to His purposes. I will build abundantly. I will give generously. I will multiply meaningfully.

My money is ministry. My prosperity is a prophecy fulfilled. My wealth is witness to His goodness. I am blessed to be a blessing, and I receive that blessing without guilt, without apology, without limitation. The same God who gives seed to the sower has given me power to get wealth. I will use it wisely. I will share it generously. I will multiply it faithfully. My financial increase brings Kingdom impact. In Jesus' name, I build."

The integration of faith and finance isn't a compromise – it's completion. You weren't designed to be spiritually rich but naturally poor. You weren't created to have heavenly treasures but earthly lack. You were designed for abundance in every realm, prosperity in every dimension, overflow in every account.

Your calling requires capital. Your ministry requires money. Your purpose requires prosperity. Not for vanity – for victory. Not for show – for service. Not for pride – for purpose.

Stop letting religion rob you of resources. Stop letting tradition trump truth. Stop letting fear disguise itself as faith. The God who owns cattle on a thousand hills wants you owning some hills too. The Father who paves streets with gold doesn't want His children begging for bread.

Your wealth is waiting on the other side of religious lies. Your prosperity is positioned beyond poverty thinking. Your financial freedom is found where faith meets strategy, where prayer meets planning, where worship meets wealth building.

Because when you align your money with your ministry, your cash with your calling, your wealth with His will – that's when financial miracles manifest. That's when money becomes holy. That's when prosperity becomes purpose.

Build wealth like heaven is watching. Build abundance, for it advances the Kingdom. Because it does. Build prosperity like it's part of your praise. Because properly positioned, it is.

Your faith doesn't limit your finances. It launches them. Now go build wealth worthy of the God you serve. He's given you the power. Use it.

CREATING YOUR LEGACY CORPORATION

It was family time on this beautiful Sunday afternoon. Dinner at my sister's house. The conversation started innocently enough, and yet, it was way overdue.

As her daughter, my niece, began talking about her senior year career plans. "I want to be a consultant like Auntie," she said, eyes bright with possibility. "Make good money, help companies, and wear nice suits."

I smiled, but something twisted in my stomach. Another generation is preparing to build someone else's empire while dreaming of crumbs from the corporate table.

That's when her younger brother, Malik, all of fifteen years old with wisdom beyond his years, asked the question that changed everything: "But Auntie, if you're so good at telling companies how to make millions, why don't you have millions? Why are you helping them build their empire instead of building your own?"

The table went silent. My sister shot him a look. But I sat there, stunned by truth delivered through teenage honesty. Twenty-two years of consulting expertise. Hundreds of millions in value created for clients.

Awards, accolades, and a LinkedIn profile that impressed. But what empire had I built? What legacy corporation bore my name? What generational wealth had all that expertise generated?

I looked at Imani, saw myself twenty-five years ago – bright, ambitious, ready to climb ladders leaning against buildings I'd never own. And I realized: I'd been playing small in a suit that looked successful. I'd been building jobs instead of dynasties, side hustles instead of legacy corporations, income streams instead of institutional wealth.

That night, the ancestors whispered through Malik's question: "Baby, your expertise was never meant to stay employed. It was meant to build employment. Your knowledge wasn't given for contracts – it was given for corporations that outlive you."

The drive home felt like a boardroom meeting with destiny. Every red light gave me time to see clearly: My consulting "side hustle" that I'd run for eight years, treating it like supplemental income instead of the empire seed it could be. The clients who paid me $5,000 for strategies that made them millions.

The intellectual property I'd created but never scaled, packaged, or protected. The opportunities I'd helped others capture while keeping myself captured in a hustle mentality.

See, there's a fundamental difference between side hustle and empire architecture that nobody teaches us:

Side Hustle Mentality: "I need extra money, so I'll trade more hours for dollars. I'll take any client who pays. I'll do everything myself to save money. I'll keep it small and manageable. I'll be grateful for whatever comes."

Empire Architecture Mentality: "I'm building an institution that generates wealth for generations. I'll create systems that scale beyond my personal capacity. I'll be strategic about growth. I'll build something that employs others and transforms communities. I'll create something worthy of the knowledge I carry."

The problem isn't that we start small – empires often begin as side hustles. The problem is we stay small, thinking small, building small, dreaming small while carrying empire-sized capabilities in our spirits.

Here's what shifted everything for me: A Legacy Corporation isn't just a business. It's a wealth-building vehicle designed to outlive you, outgrow you, and out-impact your wildest dreams.

The Legacy Corporation Blueprint has six pillars, each one essential for transforming hustle into heritage:

First Pillar: Sustainable Business Model

Recurring revenue is the lifeblood of legacy. One-off projects keep you hustling. Subscription models, retainer structures, and renewable contracts create predictable growth. My shift: Instead of chasing new consulting projects monthly, I created annual partnership packages. Same expertise, sustainable income.

Second Pillar: Community Impact Integration

Legacy corporations solve real problems for real people. They create jobs, develop talent, and transform communities. Not as charity, but as a strategy. When your business model includes community elevation, you create loyalty, purpose, and generational impact. Every person you employ, every problem you solve, every opportunity you create becomes part of your legacy story.

Third Pillar: Succession Architecture

Build like you won't always run it – because you won't. Document systems. Develop leaders. Create

operations that work without your constant presence. A hustle needs you. A legacy corporation needs systems. This isn't about exit planning – it's about building something excellent enough to outlast its founder.

Fourth Pillar: Asset Accumulation Strategy

Your business should be a wealth-building vehicle, not just an income generator. It should acquire assets: intellectual property, real estate, equipment, and investments. Every year, your business should own more, not just earn more. These assets appreciate while operations generate income – double wealth building.

Fifth Pillar: Cultural Preservation/Innovation

Honor where you come from while building where you're going. Your legacy corporation should reflect your values, serve your community, yet innovate beyond traditional limitations. It's not about abandoning culture for corporate success – it's about building corporate success that elevates culture.

Sixth Pillar: Wealth Distribution Design

Build profit-sharing, equity participation, and legacy planning into your DNA from day one. Not because you have to, but because wealth that doesn't circulate stagnates. Create pathways for employees to become owners, for communities to benefit from growth, and for wealth to multiply through sharing.

But knowing the blueprint and building from it are two different battles. So let me show you what transformation looks like in practice.

Remember I mentioned my eight-year-old consulting "side hustle"? Here's what shifted when I applied empire thinking:

Year One of Empire Building: Incorporated as LLC, then transformed to C-Corp structure for growth. Stopped accepting random projects. Created three signature service offerings. Built intellectual property from years of expertise. Hired first virtual assistant. Revenue: $87,000.

Year Two: Developed a certification program for my methodology. Other consultants are paid to learn and license my systems. Hired two junior consultants. Opened a business banking relationship for future funding. Revenue: $234,000.

Year Three: Launched an online institute teaching my frameworks. Created a passive income stream supplementing active consulting. Employed five people full-time. Acquired a small office building (business now owns real estate). Revenue: $567,000.

Year Four: Strategic acquisition of a smaller consulting firm. Instant client base expansion.

THE COMPOUND EFFECT OF CULTURAL CAPITAL

When Authenticity Becomes Your Advantage

The conference room felt different this time. Not the sleek chairs or the floor-to-ceiling windows overlooking downtown—those were the same. As I watched my colleagues enter the room, I sat across from three venture capital partners. I would normally be rehearsing sanitized corporate speeches; instead, I was thinking about my grandmother's kitchen.

"Ms. Williams, we've reviewed your pitch deck," the venture capital partner said, tapping his pen against the mahogany table. "Your numbers are solid, but we're struggling to understand your competitive differentiation. There are dozens of food delivery apps. What makes Harvest2Soul different?"

Six months ago, I would have launched into buzzwords about "scalable solutions" and "market penetration." Today, I leaned forward and said something that surprised even myself.

"Mr. Patterson, can I tell you about the last time I visited my grandmother?"

The partners exchanged glances, but I continued.

"She's eighty-three, still cooks Sunday dinner for fifteen people without breaking a sweat. Last month, I watched her season a pot of greens, no measuring cups, no recipe cards, just wisdom passed down through generations. When I asked how she knew it was right, she said, 'Baby, you can't learn this from a book. You got to feel it in your spirit.'"

I paused, watching their faces. Mr. Patterson had stopped tapping his pen.

"That's why Harvest2Soul captures what your other investments miss. We're not just delivering food, we're delivering my grandmother's kitchen, that cultural knowledge, that sense of home that algorithms can't replicate. Our cooks aren't contractors following recipes. They're cultural ambassadors carrying generations of wisdom in every dish they prepare."

I pulled up my beta test data, but now the numbers told a story instead of just showing statistics.

"Our customer retention is eighty-nine percent because people aren't just ordering meals, they're ordering belonging as well. Our average order value is forty-three dollars because customers understand they're paying for authenticity, not convenience. Our word-of-mouth marketing is sixty percent lower cost because trust travels through cultural networks faster than any advertising campaign you could buy."

The silence in the room felt different now. Heavier. More attentive.

"For twenty years. I've been translating who I am into language I thought you needed to hear, but that translation loses what makes this business work. My grandmother's wisdom isn't something to overcome; it's my competitive advantage. The cultural knowledge that built the strongest communities in America is the same knowledge that will build the strongest customer loyalty you've ever seen.'

Mr. Patterson leaned back in his chair, a slow smile spreading across his face. 'In two decades of venture capital, I've never heard anyone pitch cultural wisdom as a moat. Tell me more."

Three weeks later, Meridian Ventures led a four-million-dollar Series A round. But more than the money, they brought something I had never received before—a genuine interest in my cultural perspective. Mr. Patterson introduced me to portfolio companies specifically seeking authentic cultural insights. Two Black women executives joined the funding round not despite my authentic pitch, but because of it.

As I sat reflecting after the meeting, the funding story hit deeper each time I shared it. Each time, revealing something new.

I sat in disbelief. Shaking my head with a smile as I had talked about my grandmother's greens in the middle of a VC pitch. Not trying to be strategic, I was tired of performing. But being authentic turned out to be the most strategic thing I could have done.

I had previously struggled with code-switching in every corporate meeting, but this time I managed to nail it.

I quickly reminded myself about the boundary banking system I'd built. Never stop apologizing for protecting your money, Robin had taught me.

Same principle. I stopped apologizing for my cultural knowledge. The boundary system works because it's authentic to my values while being strategic for my wealth. My authentic pitch worked because it was both true to who I am and valuable to what they needed.

But how did I know it would work? I didn't. But I knew the alternative definitely wasn't working. Eighteen rejections taught me that pretending to be what they expected was a guaranteed losing strategy. Being myself was at least a different strategy.

I sat quietly for a moment, thinking about my own corporate experiences. The voice I used in board meetings. The way I straightened my posture was beyond comfort. The cultural references I suppressed and the validation I performed.

It finally hit me: my cultural identity isn't something to manage—it's something to leverage.

Not just leverage. It's the actual asset. Think about it. What did those VCs really invest in? Not just my business plan, they can get business plans anywhere. They invested in my cultural intelligence, my community access, and my authentic understanding of a market they can't reach without someone like me.

My phone buzzed. A text from Mr. Patterson: Meeting with three portfolio companies next week who need a cultural marketing strategy. Interested in consulting? $5K per session.

This is what I'm learning. Every time I tried to minimize my cultural identity to fit in, I was throwing away my most valuable asset. The code-switching, the cultural translation, the ability to move between worlds, that's not a burden. That's expertise that people will pay premium rates to access.

I stared at the text message, my mind racing. I thought about my own skills—navigating corporate politics, building consensus across cultural lines, reading unspoken dynamics in rooms. I'd always seen these as survival tools. What if they were wealth-building tools?

I called Robin, my mentor. "I need you to break this down for me," I said, my voice urgent. "Because if what I'm experiencing is true, I've been walking around with a fortune and didn't even know it."

Robin laughed. "That's exactly what I've been trying to tell you. And now that you've experienced it firsthand, you understand. Tomorrow, I'm going to show you how to start turning your cultural capital into even more actual capital."

The conversation lasted another two hours, but it was the beginning of something much bigger—a complete reframing of my cultural identity from limitation to asset, from burden to business advantage, from something to hide to something to monetize.

My transformation had begun. Not by becoming someone different, but by finally understanding the value of who I already was.

BECOMING THE ANCESTOR FUTURE GENERATIONS THANK

Letters to Your Great-Great-Granddaughter

I sat at my kitchen table long after midnight, a blank sheet of paper in front of me and a pen trembling slightly in my hand. The house was quiet except for the hum of the refrigerator and the distant sound of my daughter Jasmine's music drifting from upstairs.

I had just finished reviewing my financial statements—two years into my transformation journey, and the numbers still felt surreal. But tonight wasn't about the numbers. Tonight was about something my mentor had challenged me to do during our last mentorship call.

"Write a letter to your great-great-granddaughter," my mentor said. "Someone who will be born a hundred years from now. Tell her what you're doing right now that will change her life."

At first, I laughed. "Girl, I don't even know if I'll have great-grandchildren, much less great-great-grandchildren."

"That's not the point," my mentor replied, her voice serious. "The point is to understand that every decision you're making today echoes forward. Write the letter. Trust me."

Now, staring at the blank page, I understood why this was necessary. This wasn't about predicting the future—it was about claiming responsibility for it.

I began to write.

My Dearest Great-Great-Granddaughter,

I don't know your name yet. I don't know what you'll look like, though I imagine you might have my grandmother's eyes or your great-great-grandfather's smile. I don't know what the world will look like in 2124, but I know something about you that fills me with a joy so profound I'm crying as I write this.

You will never know the weight I'm carrying right now.

I paused, my pen hovering over the page. I recalled all the years before my transformation—the anxiety that woke me at 3 AM, the guilt that accompanied every boundary, the fear that I'd end up like my grandmother, dependent on family support in old age.

You'll never know what it feels like to be forty-five years old and realize you've been perpetuating generational poverty with a bigger checkbook. You'll never experience the shame of having a good job but no wealth, a master's degree but no assets, a generous heart but an empty retirement account.

You won't know these things because today—right now, at 11:47 PM on a Tuesday night—I'm making decisions that will ensure poverty stops with me and prosperity starts with you.

I set down the pen and walked over to my filing cabinet, pulling out the folder labeled "Wealth Building Journey." Inside were documents that told a story: my first investment account statement, the closing papers from my first rental property, the LLC formation documents for my cultural consulting business, the Boundary Banking System I had created.

Returning to the table, I spread them out and continued writing.

Let me tell you about the decisions I'm making that you'll inherit:

Today, I opened my first real investment account. Not a retirement account that I can't touch for decades, but an actual brokerage account where I'm building wealth I can see and use. It started with three thousand dollars—money I would have given to family members for emergencies that somehow never ended. That three thousand dollars is a seed, beloved. By the time you read this, that seed will have grown into a forest.

I smiled, thinking about the compound interest calculations my financial advisor had shown me. That initial investment, growing at an average of seven percent annually, would be worth over eighty thousand dollars by the time my daughter retired. And that was just the beginning.

Six months ago, I bought my first rental property. I was terrified. The mortgage felt crushing, and I had nightmares about tenants destroying the place. But I knew that real wealth came from assets, not income. That duplex became the foundation of something big-

ger than I could imagine then. I'm writing this letter in the kitchen of that property—I moved into one unit and rented the other. The rent covers my mortgage and creates a surplus that I invest each month.

I paused, thinking about how revolutionary that decision had been. My family thought I was crazy to move into a "rental property" when I had a "perfectly good house." But they didn't understand what I was building.

Last month, I started my consulting business. Not because I had all the answers, but because I finally understood that my cultural intelligence wasn't a burden—it was an asset. I named it Heritage Breakthrough Strategies, and I help corporations understand the markets they can't reach without authentic cultural insight. The business already generates more monthly income than my salary did five years ago, and I'm just getting started.

I looked at my business account balance on my phone. The number still shocked me. Eight months in, and Soul2Harvest had generated more profit than I'd made in any year of my corporate career.

But beloved, the most important decision I made wasn't about money—it was about boundaries.

My hand moved faster now, the words flowing from a place deep in my soul.

I created something I call Boundary Banking. I stopped saying yes to every family financial request and started saying yes to our generational future. I know my family called me selfish. I know some people stopped speaking to me. But I chose your prosperity over their comfort, and I'd make that choice again every single day.

The money I protected by setting boundaries—by saying no to cousins' business loans that never had real business plans, by refusing to bail out family members who wouldn't budge, by stopping the cycle of dependency—that money became your inheritance. The hundred and eighty thousand dollars I gave away in the decade before my transformation? I calculated what that would be worth if I'd invested it instead. Over three hundred and fifty thousand dollars.

But I chose differently going forward. And that choice means you'll grow up with choices I never had.

I stood and walked to the window, looking out at the quiet street. Two years ago, I would have felt guilty writing these words. Tonight, I felt only peace and purpose.

Returning to the table, I wrote the words that had been forming in my heart since I began the letter.

Because of the decisions I'm making tonight, beloved, you will grow up in a different world than I did. Not a different country or era—a different financial reality.

You'll grow up seeing wealth as normal, not exceptional. Business ownership as expected, not extraordinary. Financial freedom as your birthright, not your desperate dream.

You'll never wonder if you can afford college—the family education fund will cover it. You'll never stress about emergency expenses—the family emergency reserve will handle them. You'll never feel trapped by a job—the passive income streams will give you freedom to choose work you love.

You'll never feel guilty about spending money on joy because abundance will be your family's natural state. You'll never fear old age because legacy structures will mean security is your inheritance.

But more than money, beloved, you're inheriting something else: you're inheriting the blueprint. You're inheriting the knowledge that one person's courage can change everything for everyone who comes after. You're inheriting proof that generational curses can be broken and generational blessings can be built.

My vision blurred with tears, but I kept writing.

I want you to understand something. The life you're living—the freedom you have, the choices you enjoy, the security you feel—it didn't happen by accident. It happened because your great-great-grandmother loved you before she knew you. Because I chose discipline over desire, investment over immediate gratification, boundaries over people-pleasing. Because I decided that being uncomfortable for twenty years was worth it if it meant you could be comfortable for a lifetime.

So when you find these letters in the family archives, know this: every investment I made, I made thinking of you. Every boundary I set, I set protecting you. Every business I built, I built for you. Every sacrifice I made, I made loving you.

I turned to a fresh page, my hand steady now.

Now let me tell you what I need from you, beloved.

Don't squander what I'm building. Don't take it for granted. Understand that wealth isn't just money—it's responsibility. You're inheriting not just assets but mission. Not just prosperity but purpose.

I need you to be the steward of what I'm starting. I need you to grow what I'm planting. I need you to multiply what I'm building. I need you to teach me what I'm learning.

Because you're not the end of this legacy, you're its multiplication. Just as I'm transforming what my grandmother could only dream about, you'll transform what I can only imagine. Just as I'm breaking cycles that held my family back, you'll break cycles I can't even see yet.

The foundation I'm laying will become your launching pad. The systems I'm creating will become your starting point. The wealth I'm building will become your investment capital for dreams I can't even conceive.

I sat back, reading what I had written. The letter had become more than an exercise—it had become a covenant. A promise to someone I'd never meet but whose life I was shaping with every decision.

I added one final paragraph.

One last thing, beloved. When you read this letter a hundred years from now, I want you to do something for me. I want you to write your own letter to your great-great-granddaughter. I want you to tell her what you're building, what you're protecting, what you're multiplying.

Because that's what generational wealth really means. It means each generation doesn't just receive—they transform. They don't just inherit—they multiply. They don't just enjoy—they expand.

The poverty stopped with me. The prosperity started with you. But the mission continues through your great-great-granddaughter and beyond.

I love you across the centuries. I'm proud of you before I know you. I'm building for you before you exist.

Your wealth-building ancestor, Maya

I signed the letter, dated it, and placed it in a leather portfolio I'd purchased specifically for this purpose. The portfolio would hold my wealth-building documentation—my transformation story told through letters, financial statements, business plans, and lessons learned.

As I sealed the portfolio, my phone buzzed. A text from my mentor: *Did you write the letter?*

I smiled and typed back: *Just finished. You were right. It changed everything.*

"What changed?" she replied.

I thought for a moment before responding: *I finally understand that I'm not just building wealth—I'm building a legacy. I'm not just changing my life—I'm changing my lineage. I'm not just breaking a cycle—I'm creating a new one.*

Now you get it, my mentor wrote back. *You're not a wealth seeker anymore. You're a legacy builder. You're becoming the ancestor future generations will thank.*

I sat in the quiet kitchen, the sealed portfolio in front of me, and felt something shift in my chest. The weight I'd been carrying—the burden of being the first, the responsibility of breaking generational patterns—it was still there. But it felt different now.

It felt sacred.

I was no longer just trying to escape poverty or achieve financial security. I was laying a foundation that would support people I had never meet, creating systems that would function long after I was gone, building wealth that would echo through generations.

The question my mentor had posed suddenly made sense: What will your letters say? What legacy will you document?

I now knew my answer.

My letters would say: I was the one who changed everything. I was the ancestor who made the hard choices so you could have easy ones. I was the generation that broke the cycle and built the bridge.

I was the one you thank.

And tomorrow, I would wake up and continue building that legacy, one decision at a time, one boundary at a time, one investment at a time.

Because somewhere in the future, a young woman with my eyes and my determination would open these letters and understand: prosperity wasn't luck or accident or privilege.

It was love, discipline, and choice.

It was one ancestor deciding that enough was enough and tomorrow would be different.

It was me, Maya.

ABOUT THE AUTHOR/FOUNDER

COACH SHARONTINE BOTTLEY

Sharontine Bottley stands at the powerful intersection of spiritual wisdom and financial expertise—a combination forged not in comfortable theory but in the crucible of lived experience. Her journey from financial uncertainty to purpose-aligned prosperity wasn't a straight path but a winding road marked by both profound challenges and divine redirection. As a divorced mother navigating corporate America, she mastered the unwritten rules of financial systems while simultaneously discovering the limitations of success defined solely by society's metrics.

Her transformation began during what appeared to be her darkest season—facing simultaneous medical challenges, career disruption, and personal heartbreak that could have broken her spirit. Instead, these trials became the fertile ground from which her most profound insights emerged. Drawing on her background in the financial banking/community reinvestment world, Sharontine developed a holistic approach to wealth-building that honors both practical strategy and spiritual principles. She recognized that the fragmentation women experience between their faith and their finances wasn't just a personal struggle but a systemic issue requiring a revolutionary solution.

What distinguishes Sharontine isn't just her professional credentials or her personal resilience, but her unwavering commitment to creating pathways for other women to achieve breakthroughs without sacrificing their values, well-being, or presence with those they love. "True prosperity," she often says, "isn't measured by accounts alone, but by alignment—the sacred harmony between who you are, what you do, and the legacy you're building." Through her bestselling books, upcoming television show, and the **Breakthrough To Wealth** movement, Sharontine isn't simply sharing strategies; she's modeling a new paradigm of success where purpose and prosperity aren't competing priorities but complementary forces flowing from the same divine source.

WHO AND WHY WE ARE

Brand Origin Story

The world wasn't designed for women who dare to want it all—purpose, prosperity, and presence in every area of life. It was engineered to keep us fragmented, depleted, and doubting our divine capacity to thrive in every dimension.

When I found myself collapsed at my kitchen table, surrounded by medical bills, financial statements, and the weight of single motherhood pressing down on my shoulders, I wasn't just experiencing a moment of exhaustion—I was standing at the crossroads of resignation or revolution. That night, as tears mixed with determination, **Breakthrough To Wealth** was conceived not as a business venture, but as an act of sacred defiance against systems that profit from our disconnection from our power.

For years, I had walked the tightrope between ambition and authenticity, between financial stability and spiritual fulfillment, between showing up for others and honoring myself. I had mastered the corporate game, navigated financial systems designed to exclude rather than empower, and rebuilt myself after personal devastation—all while society whispered that I should be grateful for mere survival rather than daring to demand abundance in every sense of the word.

Breakthrough To Wealth emerged from my soul's refusal to accept the false dichotomy between purpose and prosperity, between faith and financial sovereignty, between serving others and honoring self. It was born from the certainty that the rolling dark periods of my life—the financial struggles, career disappointments, health crises, and personal heartbreaks—weren't punishments but preparation for a calling larger than myself.

This isn't just another brand offering hollow promises of quick transformation. This is a movement reclaiming the truth that has been systematically hidden from women, especially women of color: that everything required for magnificent, multi-dimensional success already resides within you, waiting not to be discovered, but to be unleashed.

Core Mission

Breakthrough To Wealth exists to dismantle the walls that have contained women's economic and spiritual power, creating a new paradigm where purpose and prosperity flow from the same divine source. We are not here to help women adapt to broken systems—we are here to equip them to transform those systems through the revolutionary act of stepping fully into their authentic power.

Our mission transcends conventional definitions of success. By 2030, we will guide 10,000 women to achieve purposeful prosperity—a state where financial abundance emanates naturally from authentic alignment with their God-given calling. This isn't just about creating wealth; it's about healing the generational wounds that have separated women from their rightful inheritance of both spiritual fulfillment and material abundance.

Brand Values

Our values aren't corporate platitudes framed on a wall—they are revolutionary principles that challenge the very foundation of how society has taught women to pursue success, purpose, and fulfillment.

Divine Integration Over Forced Fragmentation

We reject the artificial divides that force women to compartmentalize their identities—faith in one box, finances in another, family in a third. At **Breakthroughood To Wealth**, we honor the sacred wholeness of each woman, recognizing that true power emerges when all aspects of life flow from the same source. Unlike conventional approaches that address either spiritual growth or financial strategy in isolation, we create pathways where prosperity becomes a natural expression of purpose, where ambition and faith strengthen rather than contradict each other.

Purposeful Prosperity, Not Just Profit

Who We Serve

You stand at the intersection of capability and calling—a woman who has mastered the art of making things work, of showing up dependably for others, of navigating systems not designed with you in mind. Yet beneath your composed exterior, a divine discontent stirs. You sense the gap between what you've achieved and what you're truly capable of creating. You've followed the prescribed path—education, career advancement, perhaps marriage and children—yet something essential remains unfulfilled.

Why We Serve

The statistics tell a devastating story: women control just 32% of global wealth despite comprising half the population. For women of color, the numbers are even more staggering, with Black women owning just one cent of wealth for every dollar owned by white men. These aren't random disparities; they're the predictable outcomes of systems designed to separate women from their economic power while simultaneously burdening them with disproportionate responsibility.

Our Initiatives

Our initiatives aren't merely programs or services—they are strategic pathways designed to guide women from fragmentation to integration, from limitation to liberation, from surviving to thriving across every dimension of life.

Brand Vision Manifesto

We stand at the threshold of a great reclamation—a time when women will no longer accept fragmentation as the price of participation, when purpose and prosperity will flow from the same divine source, when the false dichotomies that have kept us contained will crumble beneath the weight of our integrated power.

The future we are creating is one where women's economic sovereignty matches their spiritual authority—where the boardroom and the prayer room are no longer separate domains but harmonized expressions of the same authentic leadership. We envision communities transformed by women who build wealth not just for personal comfort but as a vehicle for collective elevation, who create businesses that solve meaningful problems while generating abundant resources for multiple generations.

The time for incremental change has passed. The moment for revolutionary reclamation is here. Your purpose and prosperity are not separate destinations but the same sacred journey.

9 781946 566416